THE Classic Rock BOOK

EASY GUITAR

S0-DNL-995

This publication is not for sale in
the E.C. and/or Australia
or New Zealand.

ISBN 0-7935-4652-4

HAL•LEONARD™
CORPORATION

7777 W. BLUEMOUND RD. P.O. BOX 13819 MILWAUKEE, WI 53213

THE Classic Rock BOOK

STRUM AND PICK PATTERNS

This chart contains the suggested strum and pick patterns that are referred to by number at the beginning
of each song in this book. The symbols ⊓ and ∨ in the strum patterns refer to down and up strokes, respectively.
The letters in the pick patterns indicate which right-hand fingers plays which strings.

p = thumb
i = index finger
m = middle finger
a = ring finger

For example; Pick Pattern 2
is played: thumb - index - middle - ring

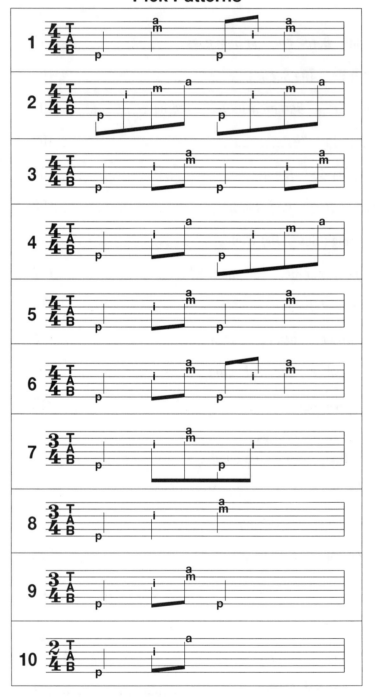

You can use the 3/4 Strum or Pick Patterns in songs written in compound meter (6/8, 9/8, 12/8, etc.).
For example, you can accompany a song in 6/8 by playing the 3/4 pattern twice in each measure.
The 4/4 Strum and Pick Patterns can be used for songs written in cut time (¢) by doubling the note
time values in the patterns. Each pattern would therefore last two measures in cut time.

All Right Now

Words and Music by Paul Rodgers and Andy Fraser

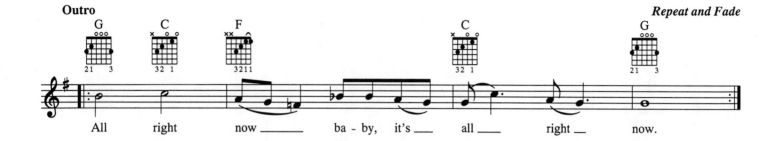

Outro

Repeat and Fade

| G | C | F | | C | G |

All right now _____ ba - by, it's ___ all ___ right __ now.

Additional Lyrics

2. I took her home to my place,
Watching ev'ry move on her face.
She said, "Look, what's your game baby,
Are you tryin' to put me in shame?"
I said, "Slow, don't go so fast,
Don't you think that love can last?"
She said, "Love, Lord above,
Now you're tryin' to trick me in love."

Heaven's On Fire

Words and Music by Paul Stanley and Desmond Child

Strum Pattern: 1
Verse
Moderate Rock

1. I look at you and my blood boils hot. I feel my tem-per'-ture rise.
2. *See Additional Lyrics*

I want it all; give me what you've got. There's hun-ger in your eyes.

Pre-Chorus

I'm get-ting clos-er, ba-by; hear me breathe.

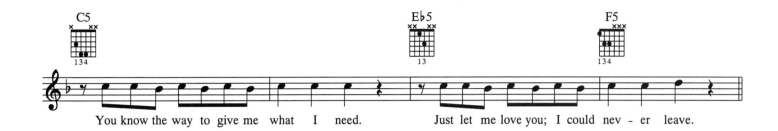

You know the way to give me what I need. Just let me love you; I could nev - er leave.

Chorus

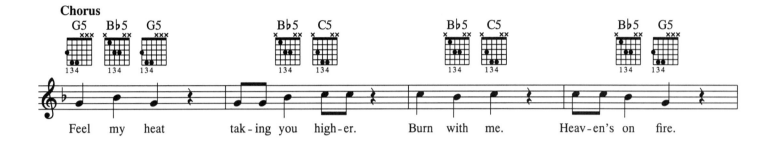

Feel my heat tak - ing you high - er. Burn with me. Heav - en's on fire.

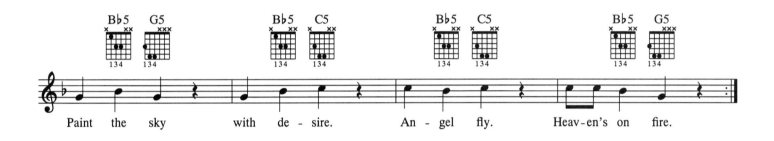

Paint the sky with de - sire. An - gel fly. Heav - en's on fire.

Bridge

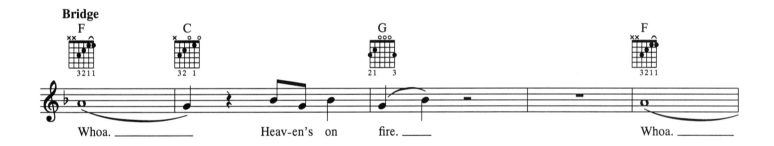

Whoa. _____ Heav - en's on fire. _____ Whoa. _____

D.S. and Fade

_____ Heav - en's on fire. _____ Whoa. _____

Additional Lyrics

2. I got a fever ragin' in my heart.
   You make me shiver and shake.
   Baby don't stop.
   Take it to the top.
   Eat it like a piece of cake.
   You're coming closer; I can hear you breathe.
   You drive me crazy when you start to tease.
   And you can bring the devil to his knees.

American Woman

Words and Music by Burton Cummings, Randy Bachman, Gary Peterson and Jim Kale

Strum Pattern: 4
Pick Pattern: 5

Chorus
Moderate Shuffle

1., 3. A - mer - i - can wom - an, gon - na mess your mind.
2. See Additional Lyrics

A - mer - i - can wom - an, she gon - na mess your mind. Mmm, ___

___ 'mer - i - can wom - an, gon - na mess your mind. Mmm,

'mer - i - can wom - an, gon - na mess ___ your mind. ___ 2. I say "A," ___

Bridge
Moderate Rock

3.

mess ___ your mind. ___

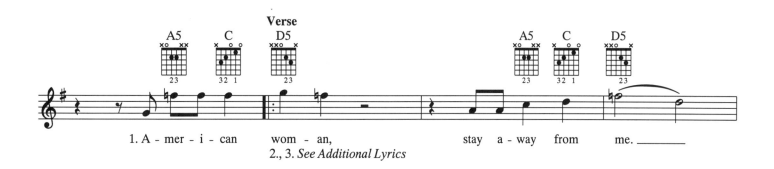

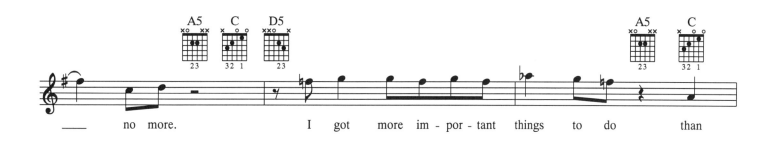

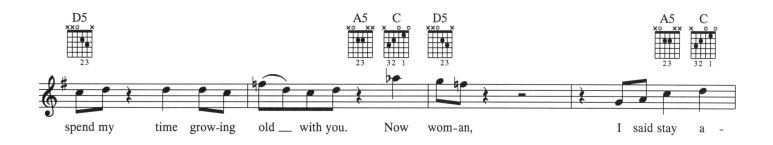

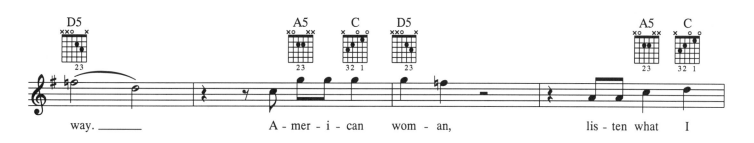

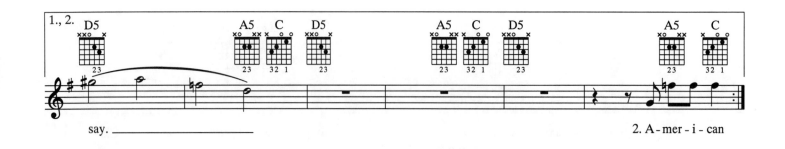

say. _____ 2. A-mer-i-can

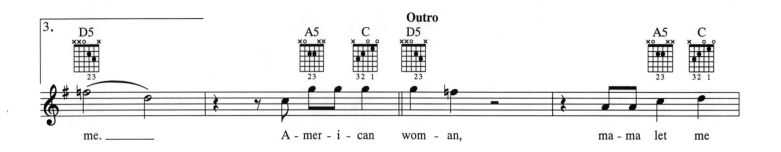

3. me. _____ A-mer-i-can wom-an, ma-ma let me

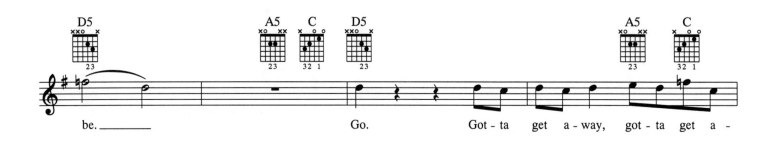

be. _____ Go. Got-ta get a-way, got-ta get a-

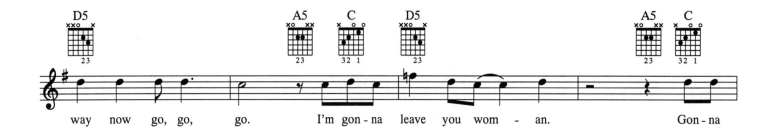

way now go, go, go. I'm gon-na leave you wom-an. Gon-na

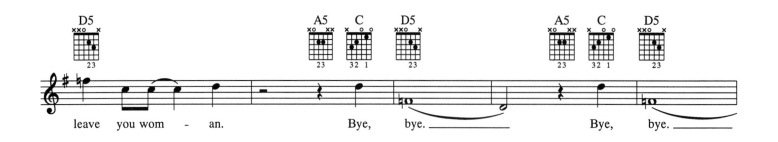

leave you wom-an. Bye, bye. _____ Bye, bye. _____

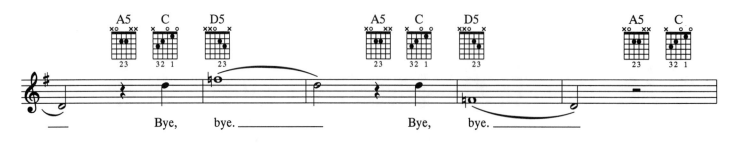

Bye, bye. _____ Bye, bye. _____

You're no good for me. I'm no good for you. Gon-na look you right

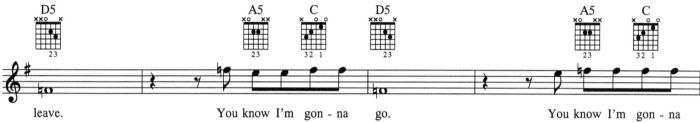

in the eye. ___ Tell you what I'm gon - na do. You know I'm gon - na

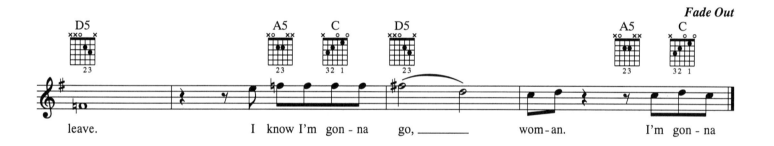

leave. You know I'm gon - na go. You know I'm gon - na

Fade Out

leave. I know I'm gon - na go, ___ wom-an. I'm gon - na

Additional Lyrics

Chorus I say "A," uh. I say "M," uh.
I say "E," I say "R."
I say "I" and "C."
I say "A," "N," mm.

2. American woman, get away from me.
American woman, mama let me be.
Don't come a-knocking around my door.
Don't wanna see your shadow no more.
Colored lights can hypnotize.
Sparkle someone else's eyes.
Now woman, I said get away.
American woman, listen what I say.

3. American woman, I said get away.
American woman, listen what I say.
Don't come hanging around my door.
Don't wanna see your face no more.
I don't need your war machines.
I don't need your ghetto scenes.
Colored lights can hypnotize.
Sparkle someone else's eyes.
Now woman, get away from me.

Angie

Words and Music by Mick Jagger and Keith Richards

Strum Pattern: 2, 3
Pick Pattern: 4

Verse
Moderately

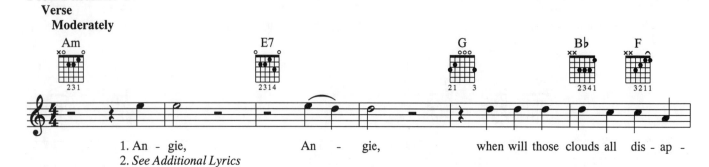

1. An - gie,   An - gie,   when will those clouds all dis - ap -
2. *See Additional Lyrics*

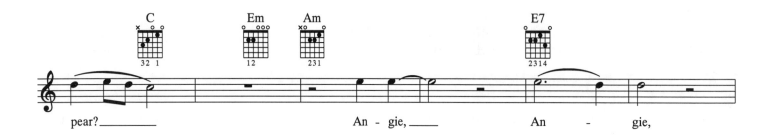

pear?_____   An - gie,_____   An - gie,

where will it lead us from here?_____   With no lov-ing in our

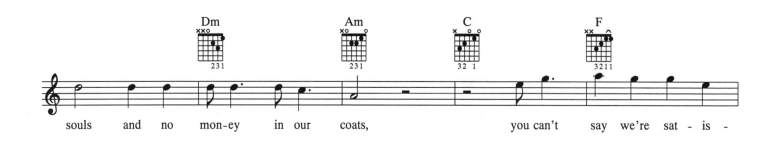

souls and no mon-ey in our coats,   you can't say we're sat - is -

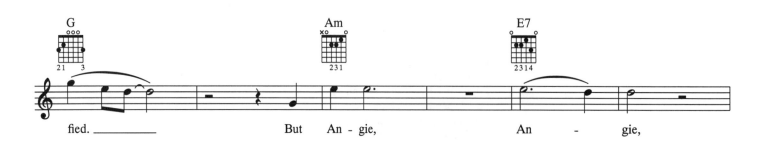

fied._____   But An - gie,   An - gie,

you can't say we nev-er tried. _____ Oh, __

Bridge

An-gie, don't _ you weep. All your kiss-es still taste sweet. I hate that

sad-ness in your eyes. _____ But An-gie, An -

gie, ain't it time we said good-bye? _____ With no lov-ing in our

souls and no mon-ey in our coats, you can't say we're sat-is-

Outro

fied. _____ But An-gie, I still _ love you, ba - by.

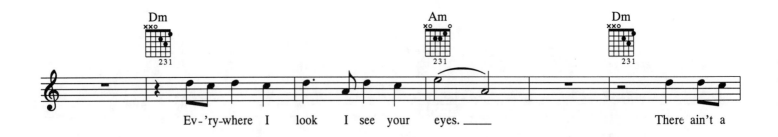

Ev-'ry-where I look I see your eyes. _____ There ain't a

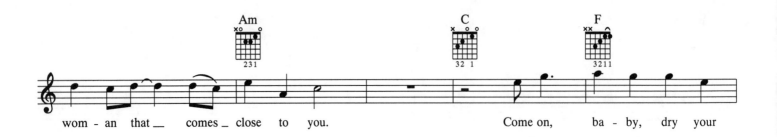

wom - an that __ comes _ close to you. Come on, ba - by, dry your

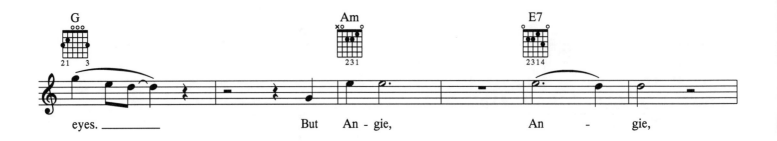

eyes. _____ But An - gie, An - gie,

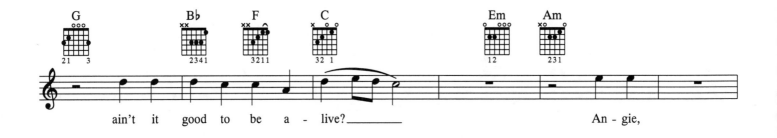

ain't it good to be a - live? _____ An - gie,

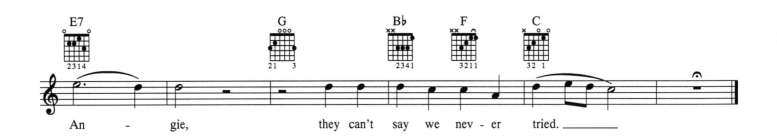

An - gie, they can't say we nev - er tried. _____

Additional Lyrics

2. Angie, you're beautiful,
   But ain't it time we said goodbye?
   Angie, I still love you.
   Remember all those nights we cried?
   All the dreams we held so close seemed to all go up in smoke.
   Let me whisper in your ear:
   "Angie, Angie, where will it lead us from here?"

Beast Of Burden

Words and Music by Mick Jagger and Keith Richards

Strum Pattern: 2, 4
Pick Pattern: 2., 4
Verse
Moderately Slow

Additional Lyrics

2. I'll never be your beast of burden.
   I've walked for miles, my feet are hurting.
   All I want is for you to make love to me.

3. I'll never be your beast of burden,
   So let's go home and draw the curtains.
   Music on the radio, come on baby make sweet love to me.

6. I'll never be your beast of burden.
   I've walked for miles, my feet are hurting.
   All I want is for you to make love to me.

7. I won't need no beast of burden.
   I need no fussing, I need no nursing.
   Never, never, never, never, never, never, never be.

Another One Bites The Dust

Words and Music by John Deacon

Strum Pattern: 4
Pick Pattern: 5

Intro
Steady Rock

1. Steve walks wa - ri - ly down ___ the street with the brim pulled way down low. ___
2., 3. *See Additional Lyrics*

Ain't no sound but the sound of his feet; ___ ma - chine guns read - y to go. ___ Are you

read - y? Hey! Are you read - y for this? Are you hang - in' on the edge of your seat? ___

___ Out of the door - way the bul - lets rip to the sound of the beat. ___

Chorus

___ An - oth - er one bites the dust. ___

Additional Lyrics

2. How do you think I'm going to get along without you when you're gone?
   You took me for ev'rything that I had and kicked me out on my own.
   Are you happy? Are you satisfied?
   How long can you stand the heat?
   Out of the doorway the bullets rip to the sound of the beat.

3. There are plenty of ways can hurt a man and bring him to the ground.
   You can beat him. You can cheat him. You can treat him bad and leave him when he's down.
   But I'm ready, yes I'm ready for you.
   I'm standing on my own two feet.
   Out of the doorway the bullets rip, repeating to the sound of the beat.

Back In The U.S.S.R.

Words and Music by John Lennon and Paul McCartney

Strum Pattern: 1
Pick Pattern: 1

Verse

Fast Rock

1. Flew in from Mi - a - mi Beach, B. O. A. C., did - n't get to
2., 3. *See Additional Lyrics*

bed last night. On the way the pa - per bag was on my knee,

man, I had a dread - ful flight. I'm back in the U. S. S. R., __

Chorus

To Coda ⊕

__ you don't know how luck - y you are, _____ boy.

1.

Back in the U. S. S. R. _____

2.

Back in the U. S., back in the U. S., back in the

*Use pattern 9.

Additional Lyrics

2. Been away so long I hardly knew the place,
   Gee, it's good to get back home.
   Leave it 'til tomorrow to unpack my case,
   Honey disconnect the phone.

3. Show me 'round your snow peacked mountains way down south,
   Take me to your daddy's farm.
   Let me hear your balalaikas ringing out,
   Come and keep your comrade warm.

Bell Bottom Blues

Words and Music by Eric Clapton

Strum Pattern: 4
Pick Pattern: 4

Slow Rock

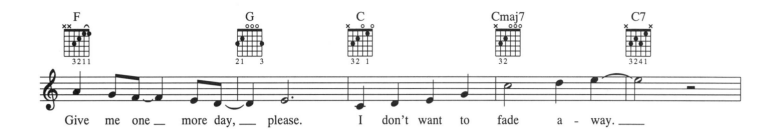

Give me one __ more day, __ please. I don't want to fade a - way. __

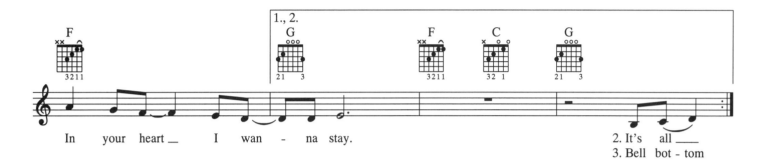

In your heart __ I wan - na stay.

2. It's all __
3. Bell bot - tom

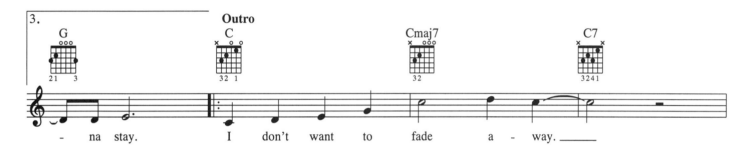

3.

Outro

- na stay. I don't want to fade a - way. _____

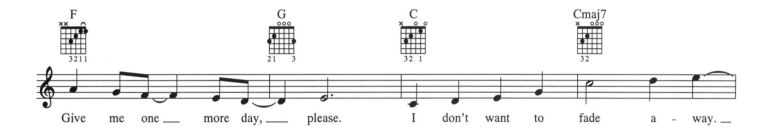

Give me one __ more day, ___ please. I don't want to fade a - way. __

Repeat and Fade

__ In your heart ___ I wan - na stay.

Additional Lyrics

2. It's all wrong, but it's all right,
   The way that you treat me, baby.
   Once I was strong, but I lost the fight.
   You won't find a better loser.

3. Bell bottom blues, don't say goodbye.
   I'm sure we're gonna meet again.
   And if we do, don't ya be surprised
   If you find me with another lover.

Blue Sky

Words and Music by Dickey Betts

Strum Pattern: 4
Pick Pattern: 5

Verse
Moderate Rock

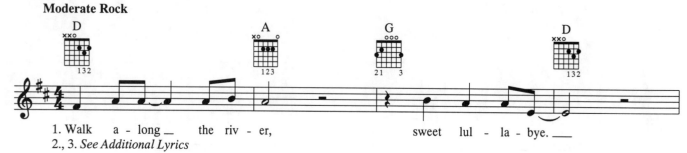

1. Walk a - long __ the riv - er, sweet lul - la - bye. __
2., 3. *See Additional Lyrics*

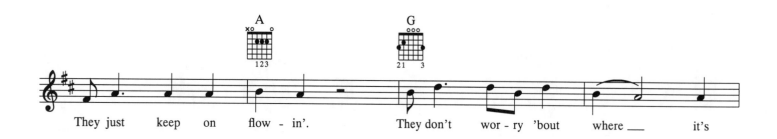

They just keep on flow - in'. They don't wor - ry 'bout where __ it's

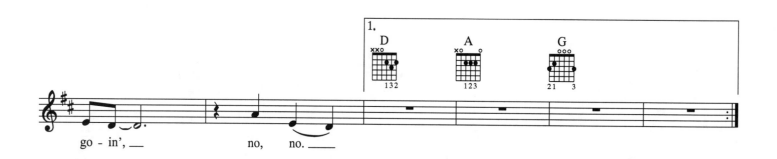

go - in', __ no, no. __

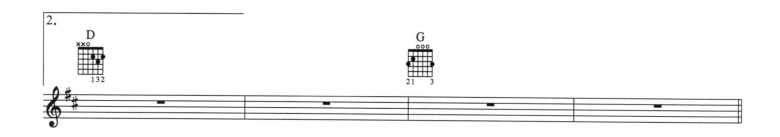

Chorus

You're my blue sky. __ You're my sun - ny day. __

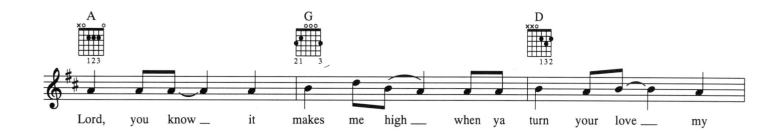

Lord, you know ___ it makes me high ___ when ya turn your love ___ my

To Coda ⊕

D.C. al Coda
(take 2nd ending)

way. ___ Turn your love ___ my way, yeah. _____

⊕ *Coda*

way. Yeah, yeah.

Additional Lyrics

2. Don't fly mister bluebird,
   I'm just walkin' down the road.
   Early mornin' sunshine,
   Tell me all I need to know.

3. Good old Sunday mornin' bells are
   Ringin' everywhere.
   Goin' to Carolina,
   Won't be long and I'll be there.

Black Magic Woman

Words and Music by Peter Green

Strum Pattern: 2, 3
Pick Pattern: 2, 3

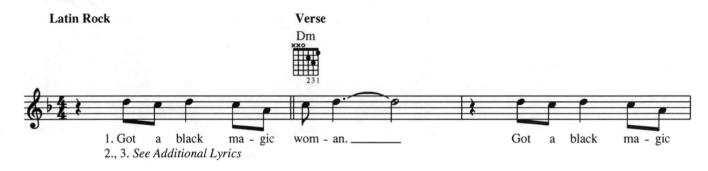

1. Got a black ma-gic wom-an. ___ Got a black ma-gic
2., 3. *See Additional Lyrics*

wom-an. ___ I got a black ma-gic wom-an,

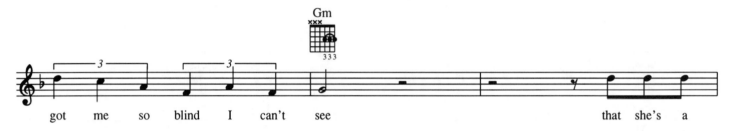

got me so blind I can't see that she's a

black ma-gic wom-an. She's tryin' to make a de-vil out of me. lone.

Additional Lyrics

2. Don't turn your back on me baby.
   Don't turn your back on me baby.
   Yes, don't turn your back on me baby,
   Start messin' around with your tricks.
   Don't turn your back on me baby,
   You just might pick up my magic sticks.

3. You got your spell on me baby.
   You got your spell on me baby.
   Yes, you got your spell on me baby,
   Turning my heart into stone.
   I need you so bad,
   Magic woman I can't leave you alone.

Bohemian Rhapsody

Words and Music by Freddie Mercury

Strum Pattern: 3, 4
Pick Pattern: 2, 3

Intro
Slowly

* Combine patterns 7 & 10.

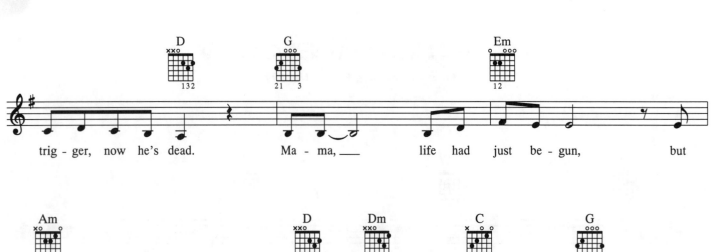

trig - ger, now he's dead. Ma - ma, ___ life had just be - gun, but

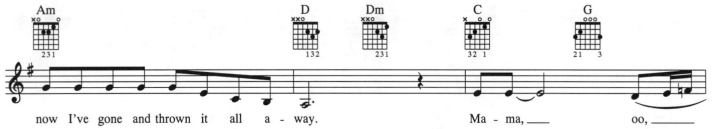

now I've gone and thrown it all a - way. Ma - ma, ___ oo, ___

___ did - n't mean to make you cry. If I'm not back a - gain this time to -

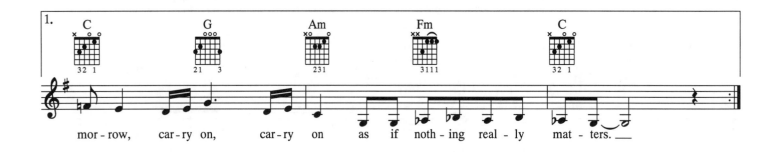

1.

mor - row, car - ry on, car - ry on as if noth - ing real - ly mat - ters. ___

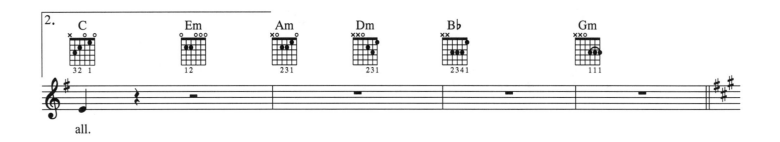

2.

all.

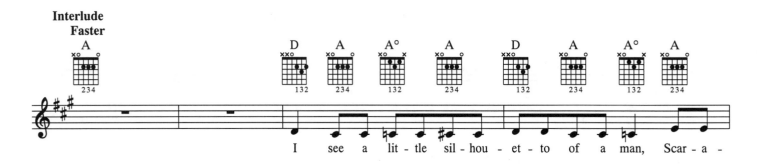

Interlude
Faster

I see a lit - tle sil - hou - et - to of a man, Scar - a -

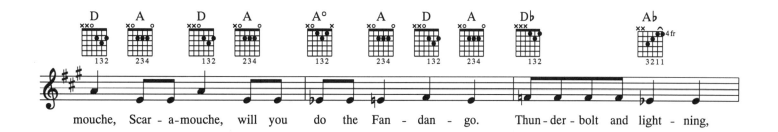

mouche, Scar - a-mouche, will you do the Fan - dan - go. Thun-der-bolt and light - ning,

ver - y, ver - y fright - 'ning me. Gal - i - le - o. Gal - i - le - o. Gal - i - le - o. Gal - i -

le - o, Gal - i - le - o fig - a - ro Mag - ni - fi - co. _____

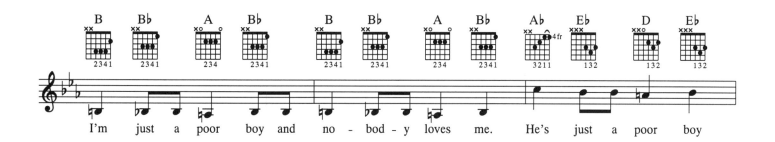

I'm just a poor boy and no - bod - y loves me. He's just a poor boy

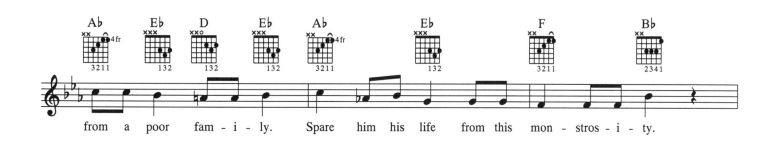

from a poor fam - i - ly. Spare him his life from this mon - stros - i - ty.

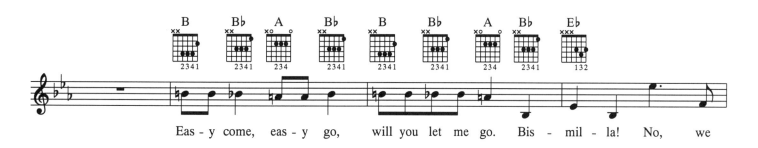

Eas - y come, eas - y go, will you let me go. Bis - mil - la! No, we

will not let you go. Let him go! ___ Bis - mil - lah! We will not let you go. Let him go! _

___ Bis - mil - lah! We will not let you go. Let me go. Will not let you go. Let me go.

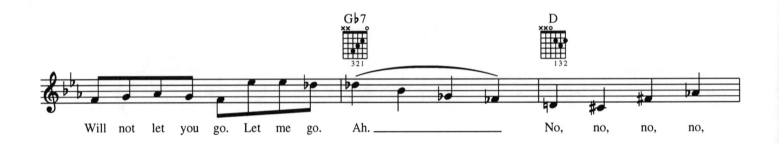

Will not let you go. Let me go. Ah. _____ No, no, no, no,

no, no, no. Oh ma - ma mi - a, ma - ma mi - a. Ma - ma mi - a, let me go. Be -

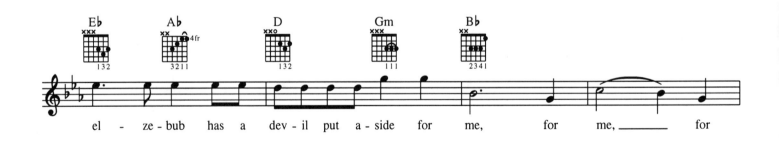

el - ze - bub has a dev - il put a - side for me, for me, _____ for

Chorus

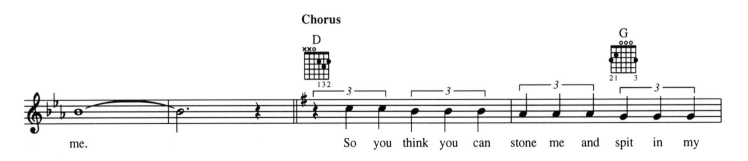

me. So you think you can stone me and spit in my

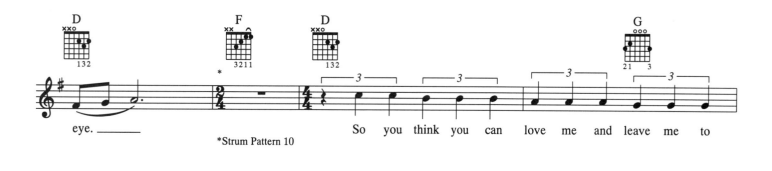

eye. _____

*Strum Pattern 10

So you think you can love me and leave me to

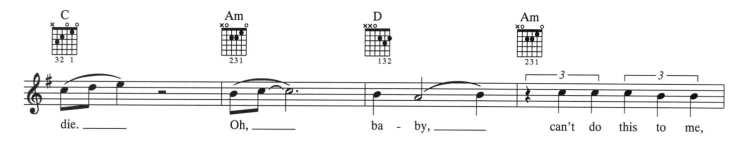

die. _____ Oh, _____ ba - by, _____ can't do this to me, baby.

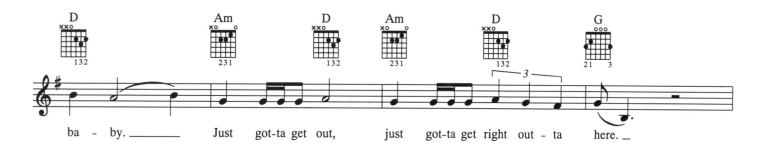

ba - by. _____ Just got-ta get out, just got-ta get right out - ta here. _

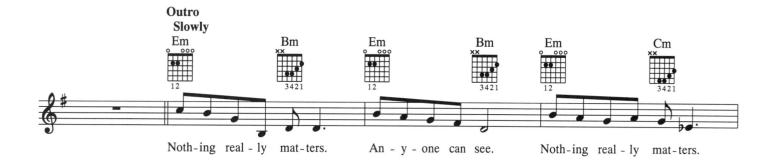

Outro
Slowly

Noth-ing real - ly mat-ters. An - y-one can see. Noth-ing real - ly mat-ters.

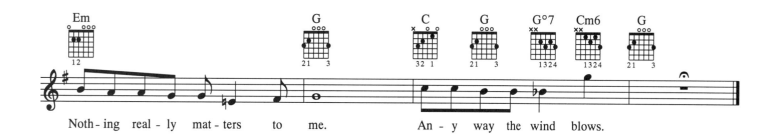

Noth-ing real - ly mat-ters to me. An - y way the wind blows.

Additional Lyrics

2. Too late, my time has come.
   Sends shivers down my spine, body's aching all the time.
   Goodbye ev'rybody, I've got to go.
   Gotta leave you all behind and face the truth.
   Mama, oo, I don't want to die.
   I sometimes wish I'd never been born at all.

Born To Be Wild

Words and Music by Mars Bonfire

Strum Pattern: 1

Verse
Heavy Rock

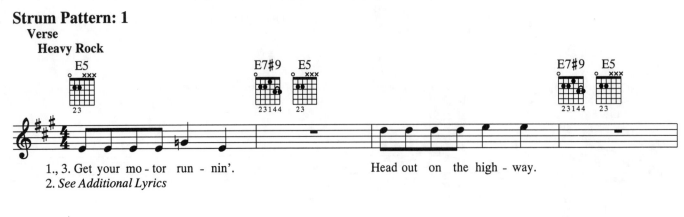

1., 3. Get your mo - tor run - nin'.
2. *See Additional Lyrics*

Head out on the high - way.

Look-in' for ad - ven - ture and what - ev - er comes our __ way. __

Pre-Chorus

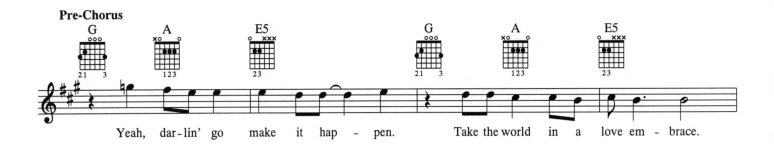

Yeah, dar-lin' go make it hap - pen. Take the world in a love em - brace.

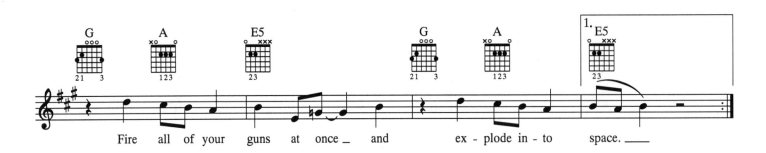

Fire all of your guns at once __ and ex - plode in - to space. ___

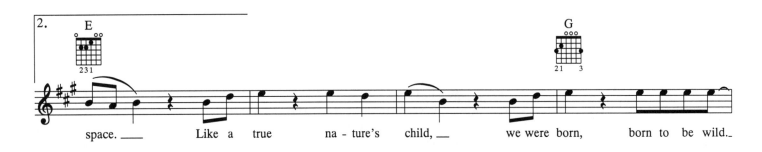

space. ___ Like a true na - ture's child, __ we were born, born to be wild. __

MCA music publishing

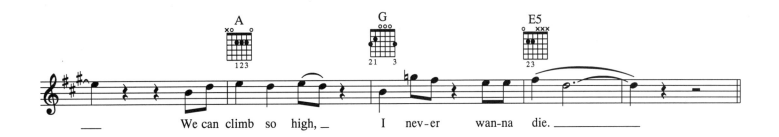

We can climb so high, __ I nev-er wan-na die. _____

Chorus

Born to be wild. _____

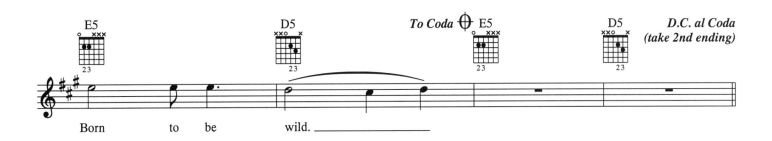

To Coda ⊕   *D.C. al Coda*
(take 2nd ending)

Born to be wild. _____

⊕ **Coda**   **Outro**   *Repeat and Fade*

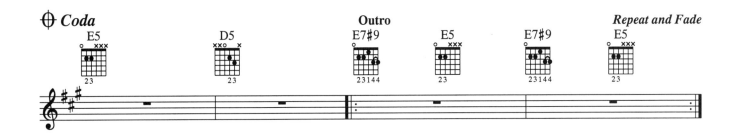

Additional Lyrics

2. I like smoke and lightning,
   Heavy metal thunder,
   Racin' with the wind,
   And the feelin' that I'm under.

The Boys Are Back In Town

Words and Music by Philip Parris Lynott

Strum Pattern: 3
Pick Pattern: 3

Verse
Bright Rock

1. Guess who just ___ got back to-day. ___ Them wild - eyed boys ___
2., 3. *See Additional Lyrics*

that had been a - way. ___ Had - n't changed, had - n't much to say.

But, man, I still think them ___ cats are cra - zy. They were ask - ing if you

were a - round. How you was, ___ where you could be found. ___

I told them you were liv - ing down - town driv - ing all the old men

Chorus

cra - zy. The boys are back in town, the boys are back in town.

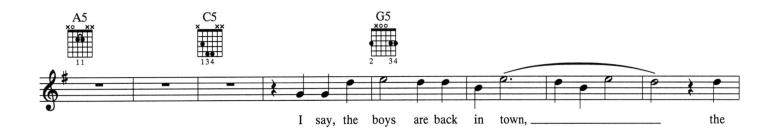

I say, the boys are back in town, _____ the

boys are back in town.   The boys are back in town, the

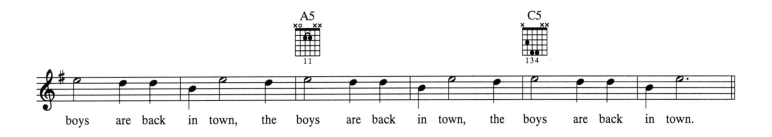

boys are back in town, the boys are back in town, the boys are back in town.

Interlude

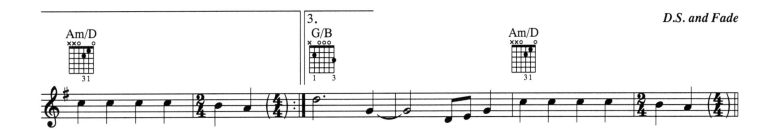

D.S. and Fade

Additional Lyrics

2. You know that chick that used to dance a lot?
   Every night she'd be on the floor shaking what she'd got.
   Man, when I tell you she was cool, she was hot.
   I mean she was steaming.
   And that time over at Johnny's place.
   Well, this chick got up and she slapped Johnny's face.
   Man, we just fell about the place.
   If that chick don't wanna know, forget her.

3. Friday night they'll be dressed to kill
   Down at Dino's Bar and Grill.
   The drink will flow and blood will spill.
   And if the boys want to fight, you better let 'em.
   That jukebox in the corner blasting out my favorite song.
   The nights are getting warmer, it won't be long.
   It won't be long till summer comes
   Now that the boys are here again.

Carry On Wayward Son

Words and Music by Kerry Livgren

Bridge

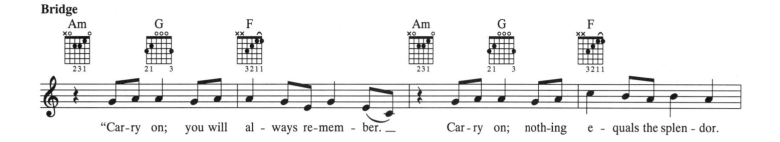

"Car-ry on; you will al - ways re-mem - ber. _ Car - ry on; noth-ing e - quals the splen - dor.

D.C. and Fade

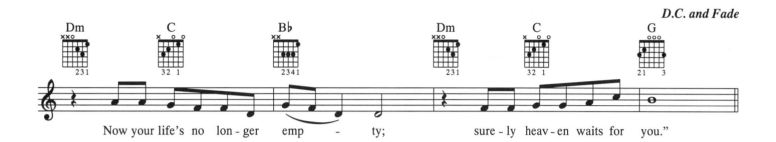

Now your life's no lon - ger emp - ty; sure - ly heav - en waits for you."

Additional Lyrics

2. Masquerading as a man with a reason,
   My charade is the event of the season.
   And if I claim to be a wise man,
   It surely means that I don't know.
   On a stormy sea of moving emotion,
   Tossed about, I'm like a ship on the ocean.
   I set a course for winds of fortune,
   But I hear the voices say:
   (To Bridge)

Cold Gin

Words and Music by Ace Frehley

Strum Pattern: 3

Intro
Moderate Rock

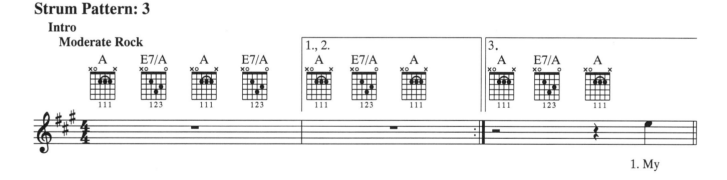

1. My

Verse

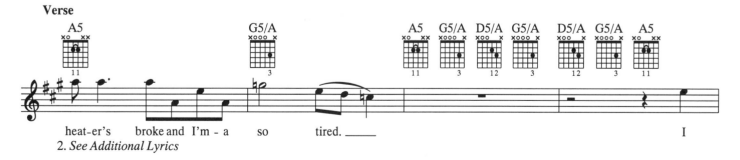

heat-er's broke and I'm - a so tired. _____ I

2. See Additional Lyrics

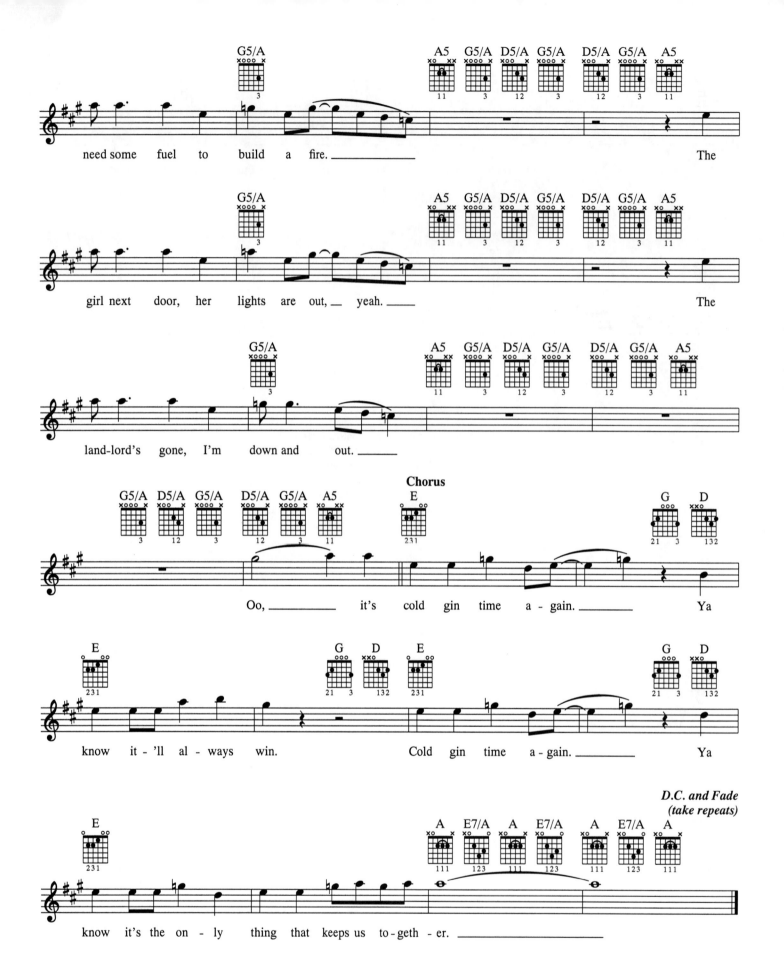

D.C. and Fade
(take repeats)

Additional Lyrics

2. It's time to leave and get another quart.
Around the corner at the liquor store.
The cheapest stuff is all I need.
To get me back on my feet again.

Cocaine

Words and Music by John J. Cale

Strum Pattern: 1

If you wan-na hang out, you've got-ta take her out, co-caine.

2., 3. *See Additional Lyrics*

If you wan-na get down, down on the ground, co-caine.

She don't lie, she don't lie, she don't lie, co-caine.

She don't lie, she don't lie, she don't lie, co-caine.

Additional Lyrics

2. If you got bad news,
   You wanna kick them blues, cocaine.
   When your day is done
   And ya wanna run, cocaine.

3. If your thing is gone
   And ya wanna ride on, cocaine.
   Don't forget this fact,
   Can't get it back, cocaine.

Come Together

Words and Music by John Lennon and Paul McCartney

Strum Pattern: 1

Verse
Slow Rock

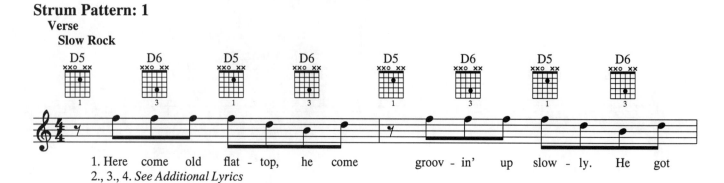

1. Here come old flat-top, he come groov-in' up slow-ly. He got
2., 3., 4. *See Additional Lyrics*

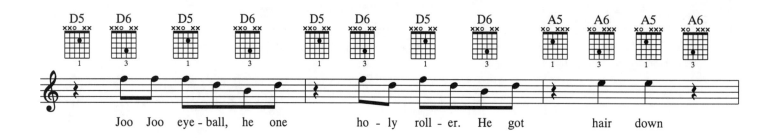

Joo Joo eye-ball, he one ho-ly roll-er. He got hair down

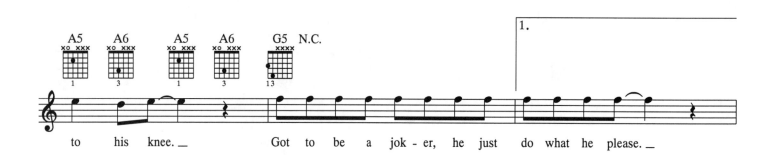

to his knee. ___ Got to be a jok-er, he just do what he please. ___

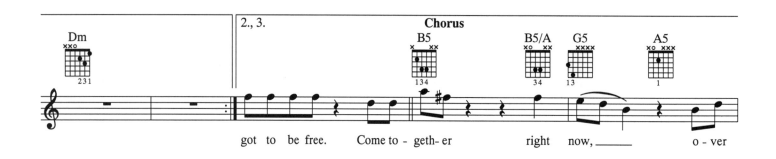

got to be free. Come to-geth-er right now, _____ o-ver

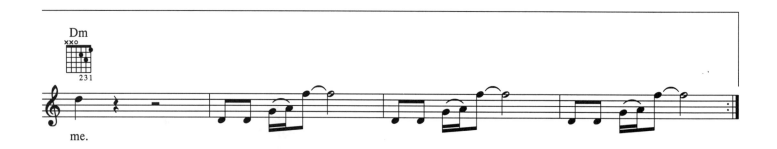

me.

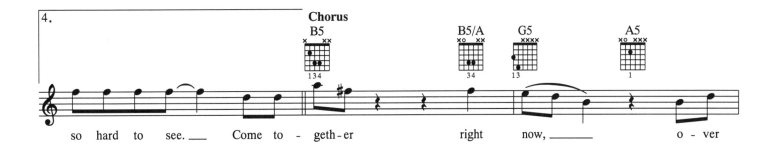

so hard to see. ___ Come to - geth - er right now, ___ o - ver

me.

Outro *Repeat and Fade*

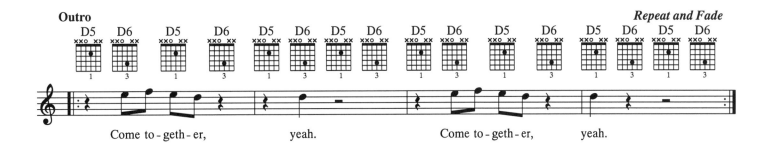

Come to - geth - er, yeah. Come to - geth - er, yeah.

Additional Lyrics

2. He wear no shoeshine, he got
   Toe jam football. He got
   Monkey finger, he shoot
   Coca Cola. He say,
   "I know you, you know me."
   One thing I can tell you is you got to be free.

3. He bag production, he got
   Walrus gumboot. He got
   Ono sideboard, he one
   Spinal cracker. He got
   Feet down below his knee.
   Hold you in his armchair you can feel his disease.

4. He roller coaster, he got
   Early warning. He got
   Muddy water, he one
   Mojo filter. He say,
   "One and one and one is three."
   Got to be good looking 'cause he so hard to see.

Crazy Little Thing Called Love

Words and Music by Freddie Mercury

Strum Pattern: 1
Pick Pattern: 3

Intro
Medium shuffle beat

1. This

𝄉 Verse

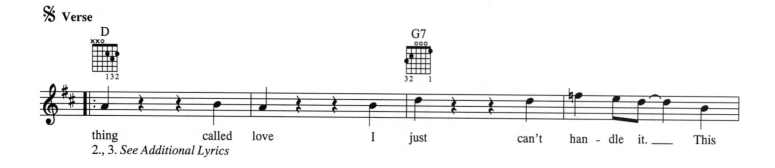

thing   called   love   I   just   can't   han - dle it. ___ This
2., 3. *See Additional Lyrics*

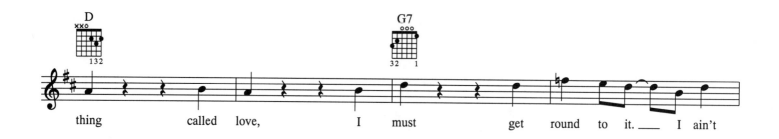

thing   called   love,   I   must   get   round   to   it. ___   I ain't

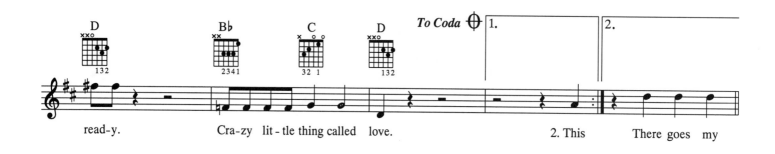

read-y.   Cra-zy lit - tle thing called love.   2. This   There goes my

Bridge

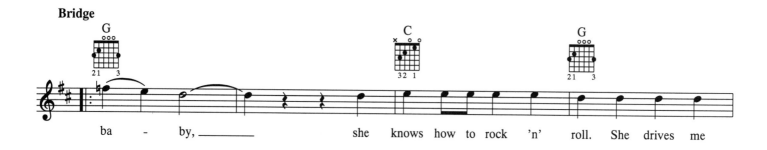

ba - by, _____   she   knows how to rock 'n' roll. She drives me

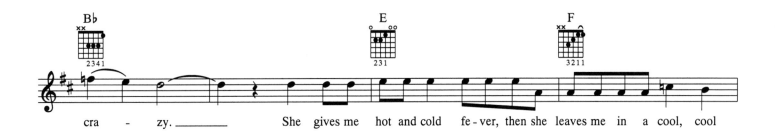

cra - zy. _____ She gives me hot and cold fe - ver, then she leaves me in a cool, cool

D.S. al Coda

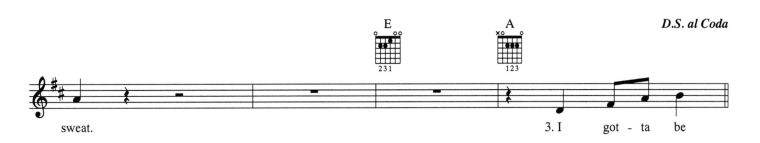

sweat. 3. I got - ta be

✠ *Coda*   ***Repeat and Fade***

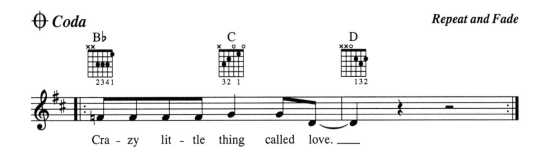

Cra - zy lit - tle thing called love. _____

Additional Lyrics

2. This thing called love,
   It cries (like a baby,) in a cradle all night.
   It swings, it jives,
   It shakes all over like a jellyfish.
   I kinda' like it.
   Crazy little thing called love.

3. I gotta be cool, relax,
   Get hip, get on my tracks.
   Take a backseat, hitchhike,
   And take a long ride on my motor bike
   Until I'm ready.
   Crazy little thing called love.

Da Ya Think I'm Sexy

Words and Music by Rod Stewart, Carmine Appice and Duane Hitchings

Strum Pattern: 6
Pick Pattern: 6

Intro
Medium Disco Beat

Verse

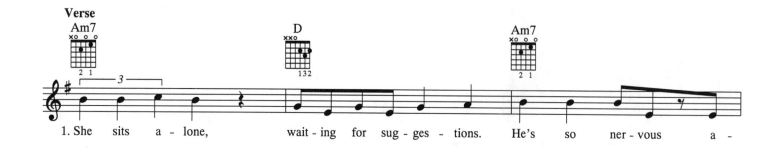

1. She sits a- lone, waiting for sug-ges-tions. He's so ner-vous a-

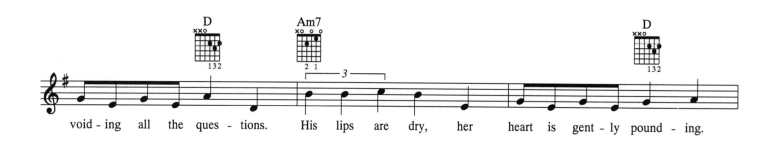

void-ing all the ques-tions. His lips are dry, her heart is gent-ly pound-ing.

Chorus

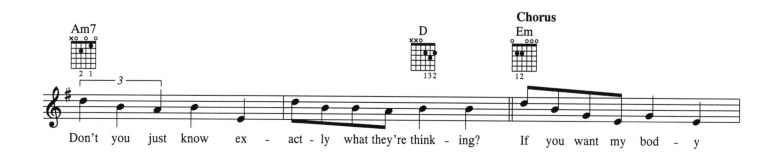

Don't you just know ex-act-ly what they're think-ing? If you want my bod-y

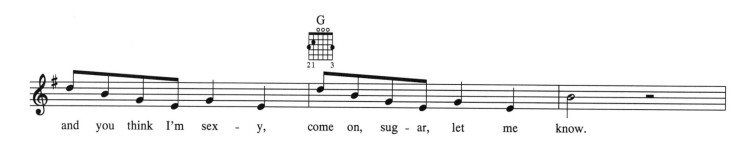

and you think I'm sex-y, come on, sug-ar, let me know.

If you real-ly need me, just reach out and touch me. Come on hon-ey, tell me

Verse

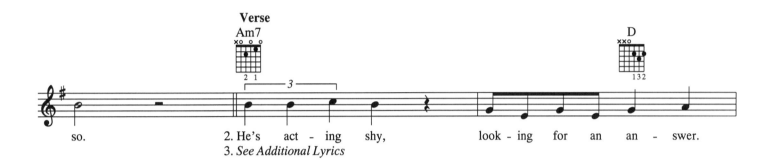

so. 2. He's act-ing shy, look-ing for an an-swer.
3. *See Additional Lyrics*

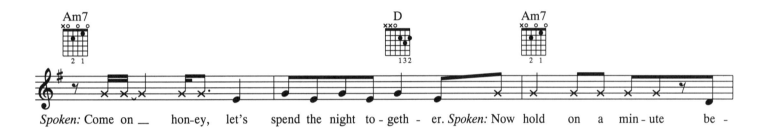

Spoken: Come on __ hon-ey, let's spend the night to-geth-er. *Spoken:* Now hold on a min-ute be-

fore we go much fur-ther, give me a dime so I can phone my moth-er.

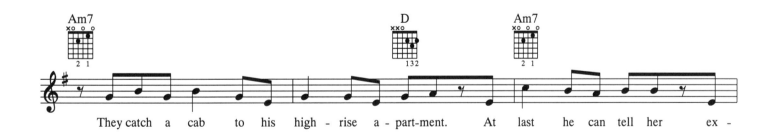

They catch a cab to his high-rise a-part-ment. At last he can tell her ex-

Chorus

act-ly what his heart meant. If you want my bod-y and you think I'm sex-y,

come on, sug - ar, let me know. If you real - ly need me,

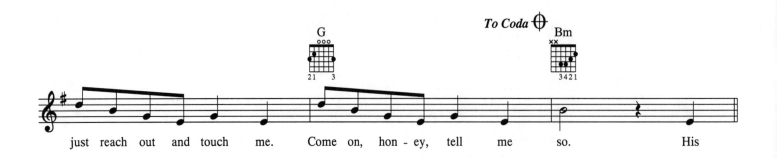

To Coda

just reach out and touch me. Come on, hon - ey, tell me so. His

Bridge

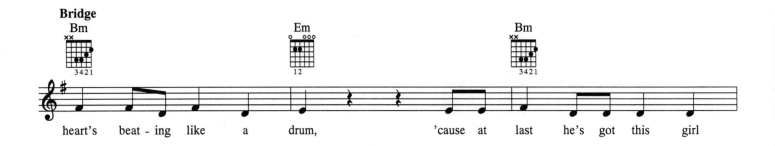

heart's beat - ing like a drum, 'cause at last he's got this girl

D.S. al Coda

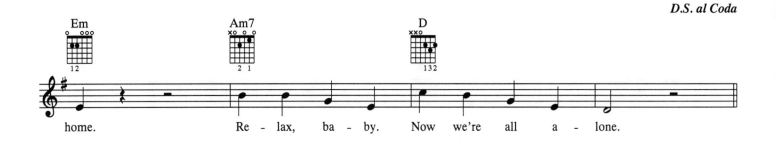

home. Re - lax, ba - by. Now we're all a - lone.

Coda **Outro** *Repeat and Fade*

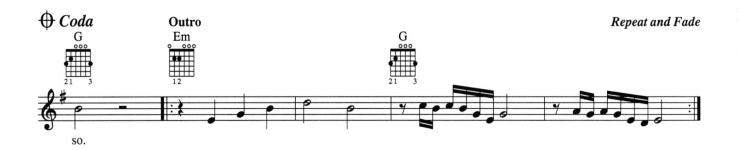

so.

Additional Lyrics

3. They wake at dawn, 'cause all the birds are singing.
Two total strangers, but that ain't what they're thinking.
Outside it's cold, misty and it's raining.
They got each other. Neither one's complaining.
He says, "I'm sorry, but I'm out of milk and coffee."
"Never mind sugar, we can watch the early movie."

Dear Mr. Fantasy

Words and Music by James Capaldi, Chris Wood and Steve Winwood

Don't Stand So Close To Me

Words and Music by Sting

Strum Pattern: 2
Pick Pattern: 3

Verse
Bright Rock

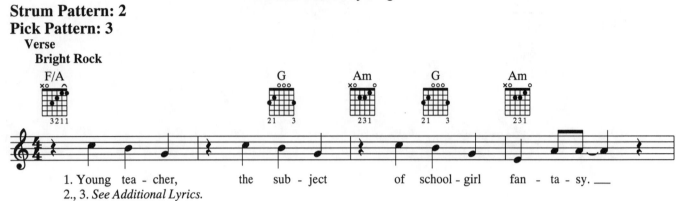

1. Young tea-cher, the sub-ject of school-girl fan-ta-sy. ___
2., 3. *See Additional Lyrics.*

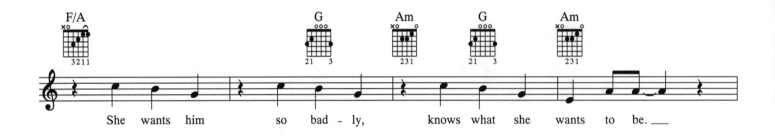

She wants him so bad-ly, knows what she wants to be. ___

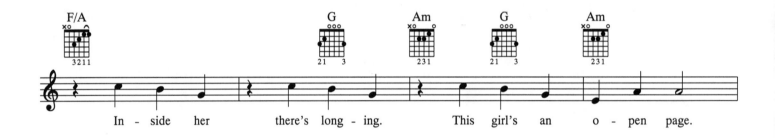

In - side her there's long - ing. This girl's an o - pen page.

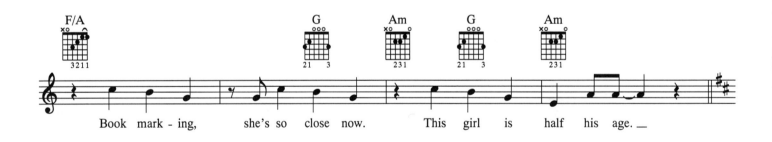

Book mark - ing, she's so close now. This girl is half his age. ___

Chorus

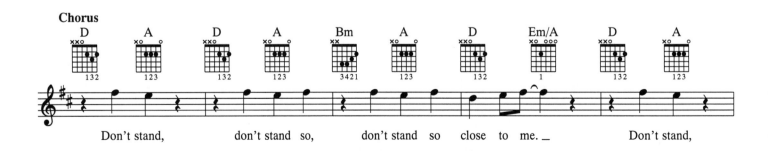

Don't stand, don't stand so, don't stand so close to me. ___ Don't stand,

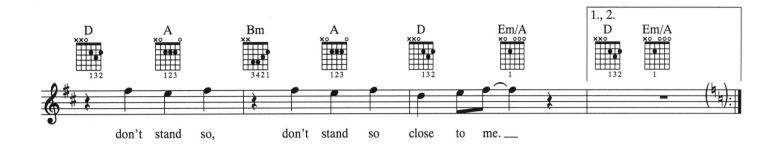

don't stand so, don't stand so close to me. ___

3. Outro

Repeat and Fade

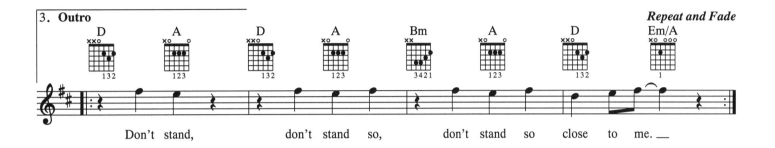

Don't stand, don't stand so, don't stand so close to me. ___

Additional Lyrics

2. Her friends are so jealous.
   You know how bad girls get.
   Sometimes it's not so easy,
   To be the teacher's pet.
   Temptation, frustration,
   So bad it makes him cry.
   Wet bus stop, she's waiting.
   His car is warm and dry.

3. Loose talk in the classroom,
   To hurt they try and try.
   Strong talk in the staff room,
   The accusations fly.
   It's no use, he sees her.
   He starts to shake and cough,
   Just like the old man in
   That book by Nabakov.

Doo Doo Doo Doo Doo (Heartbreaker)

Words and Music by Mick Jagger and Keith Richards

Strum Pattern: 5, 6
Pick Pattern: 1

Verse
Moderate Rock

stick-ing nee-dles in her arms. _____ She died __ in the dirt of an al - ley - way, her moth - er said she had no chance. _ No chance!

Chorus

Heart break-er, ___ heart break-er, ___ she stuck the pins right in her heart. _

Heart break-er, ___ pain mak-er, ___ stole the love right out of your heart. _

Heart break-er, ___ heart break-er, ___ you stole the love right out of my heart. _

Heart break-er, ___ heart break-er, ___ I wan-na tear your world a - part.

Outro *Repeat and Fade*

Doo, doo, doo, doo, doo, doo, doo, doo, doo, doo, doo, doo, doo, doo, doo, doo, doo, doo, doo, doo, doo.

Dream On

Words and Music by Steven Tyler

Strum Pattern: 4
Pick Pattern: 5

Verse
Moderately Slow

1. Ev - 'ry time that I look in the mir - ror, all these lines on my face get - tin' clear - rer. The past __ is gone; it went by like _____ dusk to dawn. __ Is - n't that the way? Ev - 'ry bod - y's got their dues __ in life __ to pay. _____ I know no - bod - y knows where _ it comes and where _ it goes. _

Dream on, ___ dream on, ___ dream on, ___ dream your-self a dream come true. _____

Dream on, ___ dream on, ___ dream on ___ and dream un - til your dream comes true.

Dream on, ___ dream on, ___ dream on, ___

dream on. ___ Dream on, ___ dream on, ___ dream on, ___ ah. _____

D.S. and Fade

Dude (Looks Like A Lady)

Words and Music by Steven Tyler, Joe Perry and Desmond Child

Strum Pattern: 1

Da, da, da, da, dude looks like a la - dy. 1. Cruised in - to a bar on the shore.

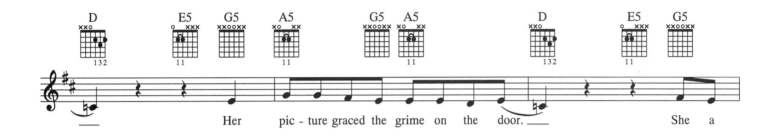

Her pic - ture graced the grime on the door. ___ She a

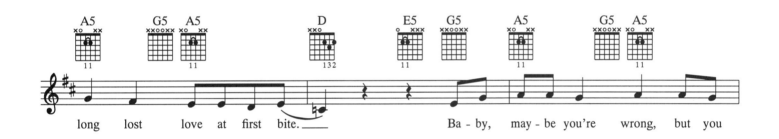

long lost love at first bite. ___ Ba - by, may - be you're wrong, but you

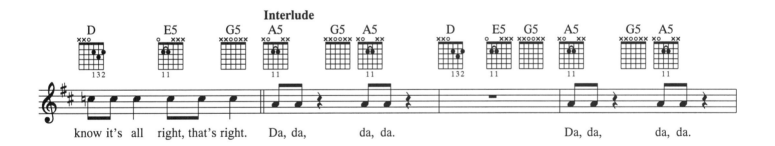

know it's all right, that's right. Da, da, da, da. Da, da, da, da.

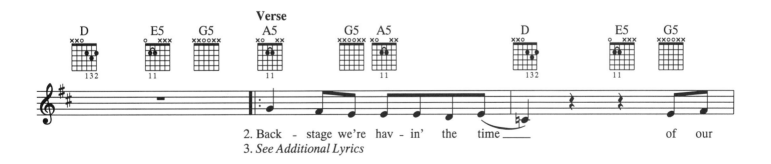

2. Back - stage we're hav - in' the time ___ of our
3. *See Additional Lyrics*

Turn the oth-er cheek, dear. __ Do me, do me,

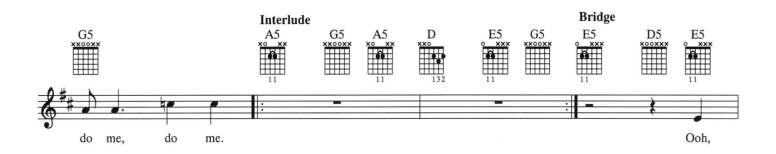

Interlude   **Bridge**

do me, do me. Ooh,

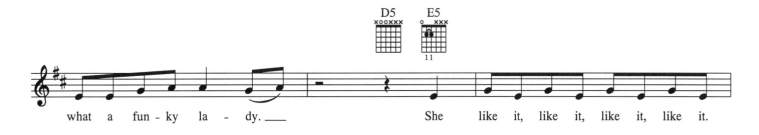

what a fun-ky la-dy. ___ She like it, like it, like it, like it.

Ooh, he was a la-dy. ___

Outro Chorus   *Repeat and Fade*

Yeah! _____ Da, da, da, da, dude looks like a la-dy. __

Additional Lyrics

3. So never judge a book by its cover,
Or who you gonna love by your lover.
Sayin' love put me wise to her love in disguise.
She had the body of a Venus,
Lord, imagine my surprise.

Dust In The Wind

Words and Music by Kerry Livgren

Strum Pattern: 1, 3
Pick Pattern: 2, 4

Intro

Moderate Ballad

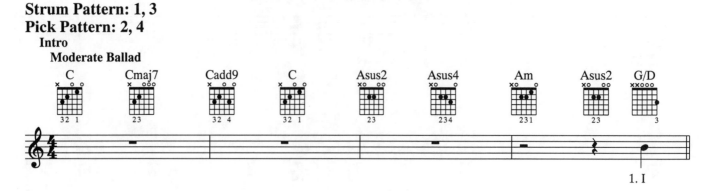

1. I

Verse

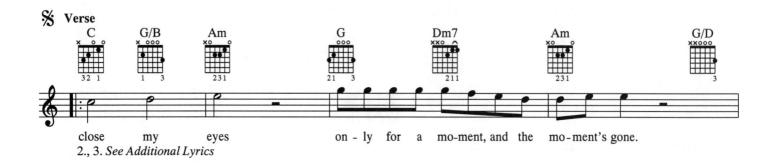

close my eyes only for a mo-ment, and the mo-ment's gone.

2., 3. See Additional Lyrics

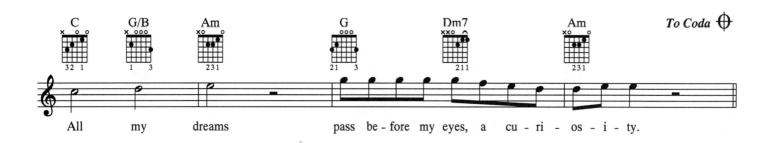

All my dreams pass be-fore my eyes, a cu-ri-os-i-ty.

To Coda

Chorus

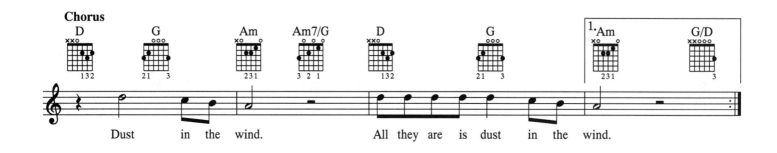

Dust in the wind. All they are is dust in the wind.

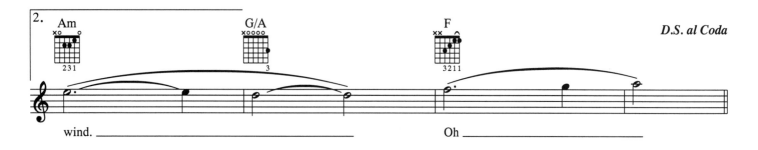

D.S. al Coda

wind. _____ Oh _____

⊕ *Coda*
Chorus

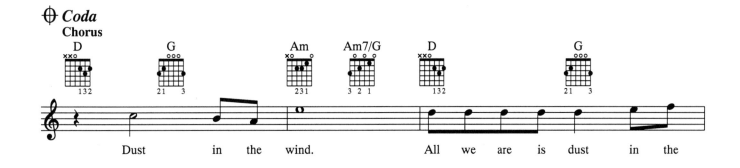

Dust   in   the   wind.   All   we   are   is   dust   in   the

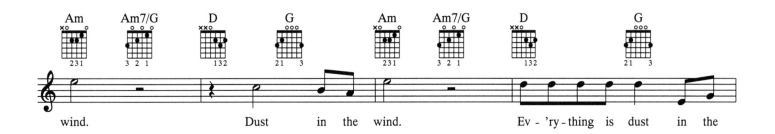

wind.   Dust   in   the   wind.   Ev - 'ry - thing   is   dust   in   the

Outro   *Repeat and Fade*

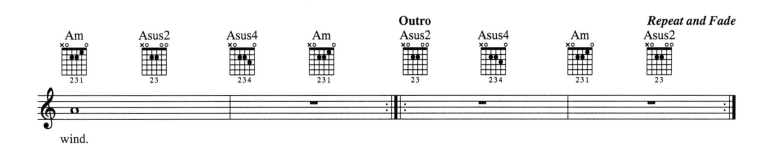

wind.

Additional Lyrics

2. Same old song.
   Just a drop of water in an endless sea.
   All we do
   Crumbles to the ground though we refuse to see.

3. Don't hang on.
   Nothing lasts forever but the earth and sky.
   It slips away.
   And all your money won't another minute buy.

Feelin' Alright

Words and Music by Dave Mason

Strum Pattern: 1
Pick Pattern: 1

Verse
Moderately Fast Rock

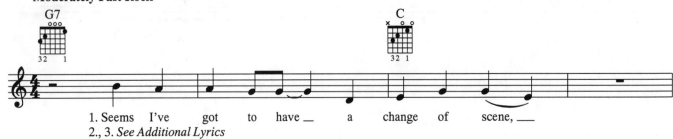

1. Seems I've got to have ___ a change of scene, ___
2., 3. *See Additional Lyrics*

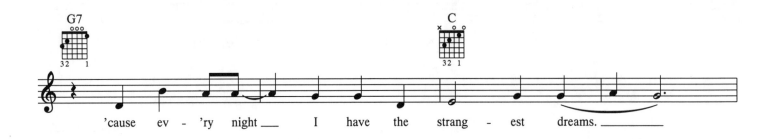

'cause ev - 'ry night ___ I have the strang - est dreams. ___

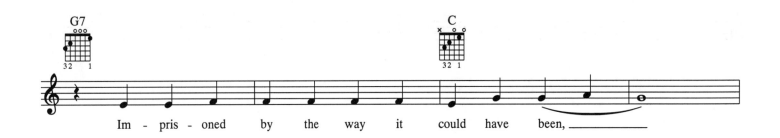

Im - pris - oned by the way it could have been, ___

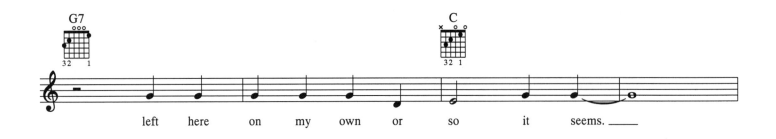

left here on my own or so it seems. ___

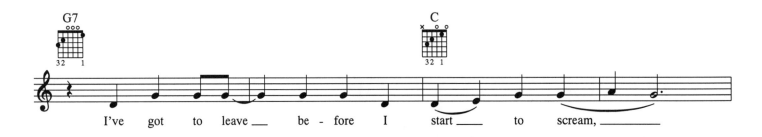

I've got to leave ___ be - fore I start ___ to scream, ___

but some-one's locked the door __ and took the key. _____ You feel-in'

%S **Chorus**

al - right?   Oh,   hoh!   I'm not feel-in' too

good my - self!   Oh,   hoh!   Well, you feel-in' al - right?

Oh,   hoh!   I'm not feel-in' too   good my - self!

1., 2.   **3.**   *D.S. and Fade*

Oh,   hoh!   hoh!   You feel-in'

Additional Lyrics

2. Well, boy you sure took me for one big ride.
   And even now I sit and wonder why,
   That when I think of you, I start to cry.
   I just can't waste my time, I must keep dry.
   Gotta stop believin' in all your lies.
   'Cause there's too much to do before I die.

3. Don't get too lost in all I say.
   Though at the time I really felt that way.
   But that was then, now it's today.
   I can't get off, so I'm here to stay.
   Till someone comes along and takes my place,
   With a diff'rent name, and yes, a diff'rent face.

Fly Like An Eagle

Words and Music by Steve Miller

Strum Pattern: 2
Pick Pattern: 2

Intro
Moderate Rock

Tick, tock, tick, doo, doo, doo, doo. 1.,3. Time keeps on slip-pin', slip-pin', slip-pin', in-to the fut-

-ture. Time keeps on slip-pin', slip-pin', slip-pin', in-to the fu-

Chorus

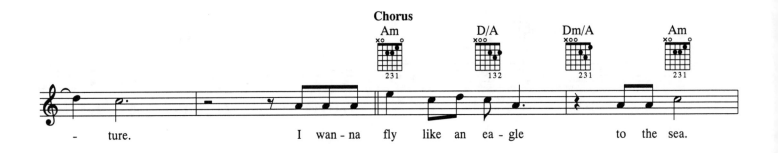

-ture. I wan-na fly like an ea-gle to the sea.

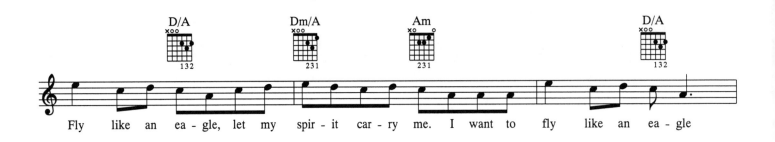

Fly like an ea-gle, let my spir-it car-ry me. I want to fly like an ea-gle

To Coda ⊕

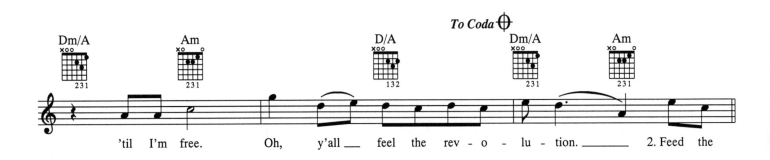

'til I'm free. Oh, y'all ___ feel the rev-o-lu-tion. ___ 2. Feed the

ba - bies who don't have e - nough __ to eat. Shoe the child - ren with no

shoes on their feet. House the peo - ple liv - in' in the street. __

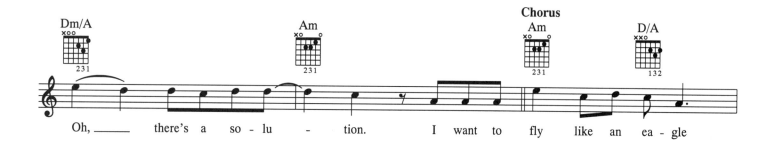

Oh, _____ there's a so - lu - tion. I want to fly like an ea - gle

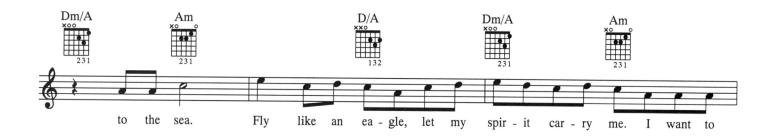

to the sea. Fly like an ea - gle, let my spir - it car - ry me. I want to

D.S. al Coda

fly like an ea - gle 'til I'm free. Right __ through the rev - o - lu - tion. _____

Repeat and Fade

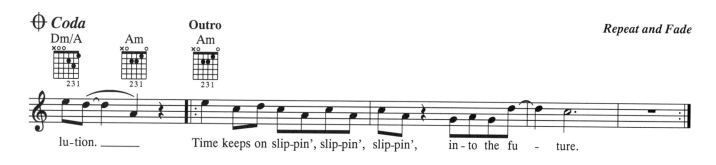

lu - tion. _____ Time keeps on slip-pin', slip-pin', slip-pin', in - to the fu - ture.

Foreplay/Long Time (Long Time)

Words and Music by Tom Scholz

Strum Pattern: 3
Pick Pattern: 3

Intro
Moderate Rock

Additional Lyrics

2. Well, I get so lonely
When I am without you.
But in my mind, deep in my mind,
I can't forget about you, whoa.
Good times and places that remind me, yeah.
I'm tryin' to forget your name
And leave it all behind me.
They're coming back to find me.

3. It's been such a long time,
I think I should be going, yeah.
Uh, time doesn't wait for me,
It keeps on going.
There's a long road
I got to stay in time with, yeah.
I've got to keep on chasin' that dream
Though I may never find it.
I'm always just behind a bit.

Forever Man

Words and Music by Jerry Lynn Williams

Strum Pattern: 3
Pick Pattern: 4

Verse

Moderate Rock

Free Bird

Words and Music by Allen Collins and Ronnie Van Zant

Strum Pattern: 2
Pick Pattern: 2

Additional Lyrics

2. Bye, bye baby its been a sweet love,
   Though this feeling I can't change.
   But please don't take it so badly,
   'Cause the Lord knows I'm to blame

Funk #49

Words and Music by Joe Walsh, Dale Peters and Jim Fox

Strum Pattern: 2
Pick Pattern: 1

Verse
Funky Rock

1. Sleep all day, out all night, I know where you're go - in'.
2., 3. *See Additional Lyrics*

I don't think that's act - in' right, you don't think it's show - in'.

Interlude

play 3 times

1.
2. *D.C. (2nd Verse)*
D.C. and Fade
(3rd Verse)

Additional Lyrics

2. Jumpin' up, fallin' down,
   Don't misunderstand me.
   You don't think that I know your plan;
   What you try'n' to hand me?

3. Out all night, sleep all day,
   I know what you're doin'.
   If you're gonna act this way,
   I think there's trouble brewin'.

MCA music publishing

Gimme Three Steps

Words and Music by Allen Collins and Ronnie Van Zant

Strum Pattern: 1
Pick Pattern: 1

Bright Rock Verse

1. I was cut-ting the rug __ down at a place called The Jug __ with a
2., 3. *See Additional Lyrics*

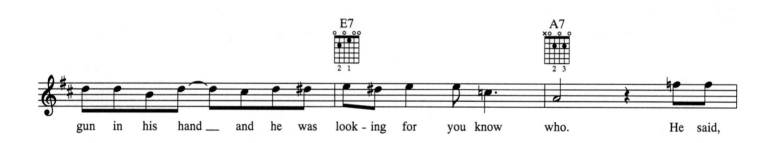

girl named __ Lin - da Lu, ___ when __ in walked a man __ with a

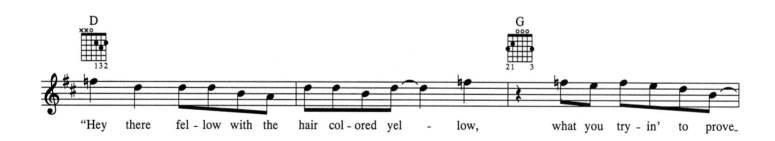

gun in his hand __ and he was look - ing for you know who. He said,

"Hey there fel - low with the hair col - ored yel - low, what you try - in' to prove __

— 'cause that's my wom - an there __ and I'm a man who __ cares __ and this

MCA music publishing

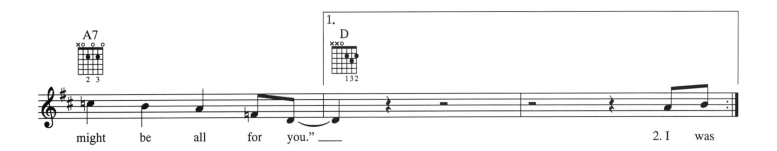

might be all for you." ___   2. I was

Chorus

___   Oh, won't you gim-me three steps, gim-me three steps mis - ter, gim-me

three steps to - ward the door? ___   Gim - me three steps, gim - me

D.S. (Fade on Chorus)

three steps, mis - ter, and you'll nev - er see me no more. ___   3. The

---

Additional Lyrics

2. I was scared and fearing for my life,
   I was shakin' like a leaf on a tree,
   'Cause he was lean, mean, big and bad, Lord,
   Pointin' that gun at me.
   Oh, wait a minute mister, I didn't even kiss her;
   Don't want no trouble with you.
   And I know you don't owe me, but I wish you'd let me
   Ask one favor of you.

3. The crowd cleared away, and I began to pray,
   And the water fell on the floor.
   And I'm tellin' you, son, it ain't no fun
   Staring straight down a forty four.
   Well, he turned and screamed at Linda Lu,
   That's the break I was looking for,
   And you could hear me screaming a mile away
   As I was headed out toward the door.

Happy Jack

Words and Music by Peter Townshend

Strum Pattern: 1
Pick Pattern: 1

Verse
Moderate Rock

*Combine patterns 9 & 10 for 5/4 throughout.

1. Hap-py Jack was-n't old but he was a man.   He

lived in the sand at the Isle of Man.   2. The

Verse

kids would all sing, he would sing the wrong key.   So they rode on his head in their fur-ry

don-key.   The

Chorus

kids can't hurt ___ Jack.   They try, try, try.   They drop things on his back   and

lie,   lie,   lie,   lie,   lie. ___   3. They

Heartbreaker

Words and Music by Paul Rodgers

Strum Pattern: 1

1. Your love is like a tid-al wave _____ spin-nin' o-ver my
2. *See Additional Lyrics*

head. _____ Drown-in' me in your prom-is-es _____

that are left un-said. _____ You're the right kind of

sin-ner to re-lease my in-ner fan-ta-sy. _____

The in-vin-ci-ble win-ner, and you know that you were

born to be. _____ You're a heart-break-er, dream mak-er,

love tak - er. Don't you mess a - round with me. You're a heart - break - er,

To Coda ⊕

dream mak - er, love tak - er. Don't you mess a - round, ___ no, no, no.

1. 2. *D.S. al Coda*

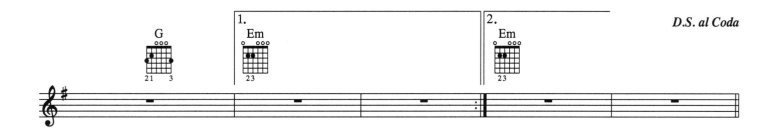

⊕ *Coda* Outro *Repeat and Fade*

mess a - round with me. You're a heart - break - er, dream mak - er,

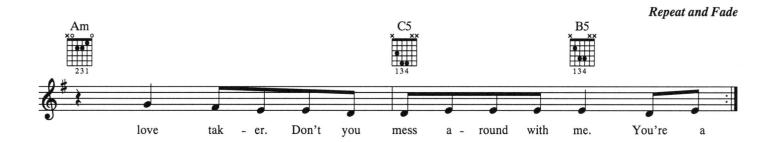

love tak - er. Don't you mess a - round with me. You're a

Additional Lyrics

2. Your love has set my soul on fire,
   Burnin' out of control.
   You taught me the ways of desire.
   Now it's taken its toll.

Helter Skelter

Words and Music by John Lennon and Paul McCartney

Strum Pattern: 3
Pick Pattern: 3

Intro
Moderate Rock

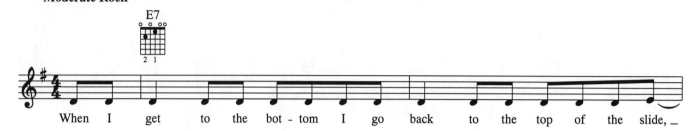

When I get to the bot-tom I go back to the top of the slide, __

__ where I stop and I turn, and I go for a ride, __ till I get to the

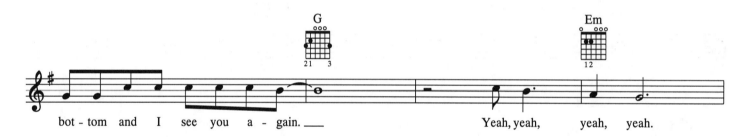

bot-tom and I see you a-gain. __ Yeah, yeah, yeah, yeah.

Verse

1. But do you, don't you want me to love you? I'm

com-ing down fast but I'm miles a-bove __ you.

Tell me, tell me, tell __ me, come on tell me the an-swer. __ Well you

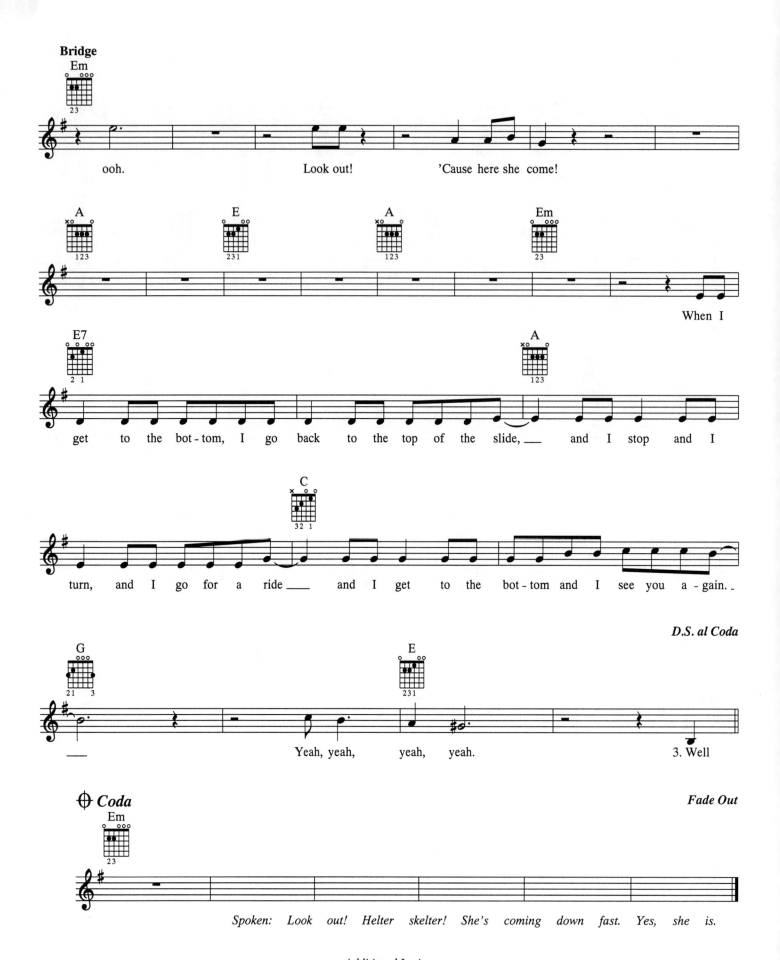

Spoken: Look out! Helter skelter! She's coming down fast. Yes, she is.

Additional Lyrics

3. Well do you, don't you want me to make you?
   I'm coming down fast but don't let me break you.
   Tell me, tell me, tell me the answer.
   You may be a lover but you ain't no dancer.

Hit Me With Your Best Shot

Words and Music by Eddie Schwartz

Strum Pattern: 3
Pick Pattern: 3
Verse
Medium Rock

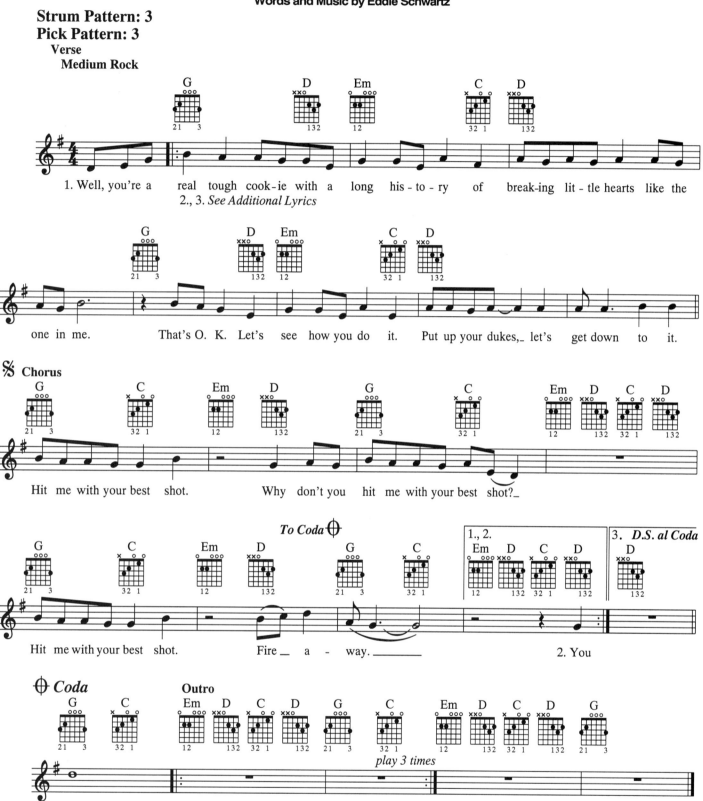

Additional Lyrics

2. You come on with a come on.
You don't fight fair.
But that's O.K. See if I care.
Knock me down. It's all in vain.
I'll get right back on my feet again.

3. Well, you're a real tough cookie with a long history.
Of breaking little hearts like the one in me.
Before I put another notch in my lipstick case,
You better make sure you put me in my place.

I Am The Walrus

Words and Music by John Lennon and Paul McCartney

Strum Pattern: 4
Pick Pattern: 5

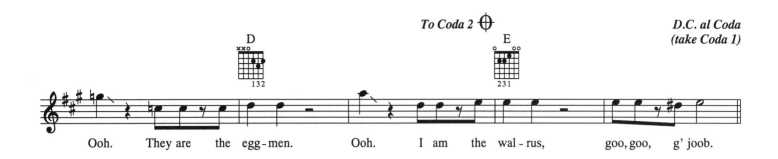

Ooh. They are the egg-men. Ooh. I am the wal-rus, goo, goo, g' joob.

⊕ *Coda 1*

I'm cry - ing I'm cry - ing.

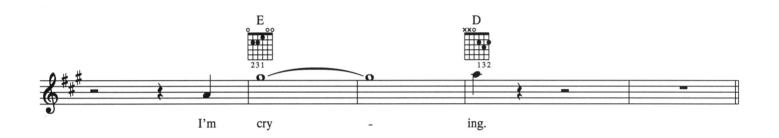

I'm cry - ing.

Verse

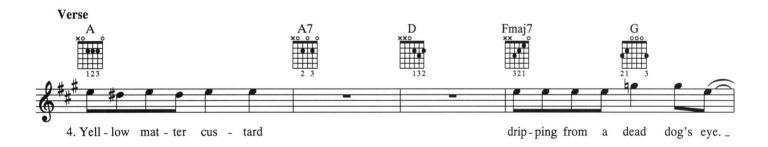

4. Yell - low mat - ter cus - tard drip-ping from a dead dog's eye. _

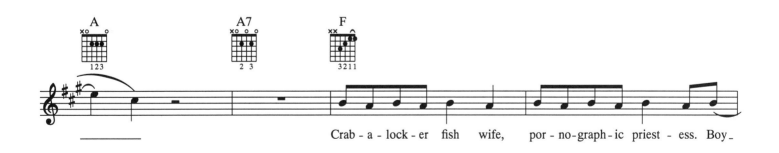

_____ Crab - a - lock - er fish wife, por - no-graph - ic priest - ess. Boy _

___ you been a naugh - ty girl, ___ you let your knick - ers down. _ I am the

Chorus

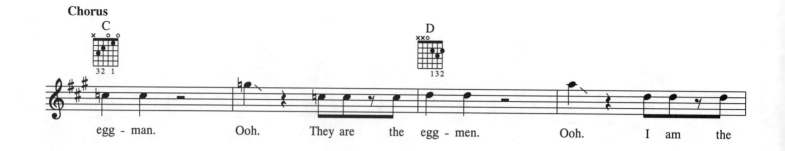

egg - man.   Ooh.   They are   the   egg - men.   Ooh.   I   am   the

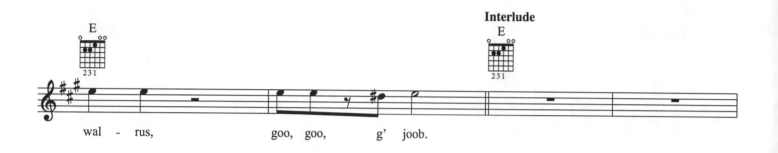

wal - rus,   goo, goo,   g' joob.

Interlude

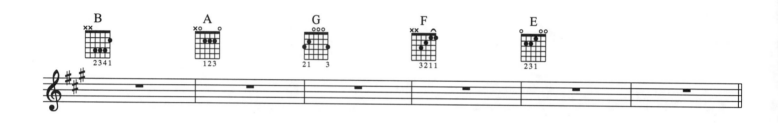

Bridge

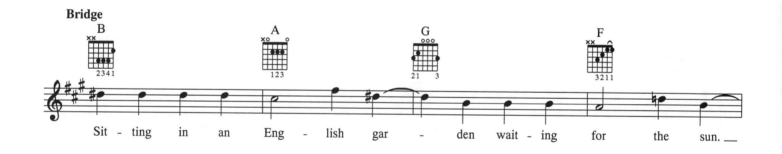

Sit - ting   in   an   Eng - lish   gar - den   wait - ing   for   the   sun. __

__   If   the   sun   don't   come, __   you   get   a   tan   from   stand -

- ing   in   the   Eng - lish   rain. __   I   am   the

Chorus

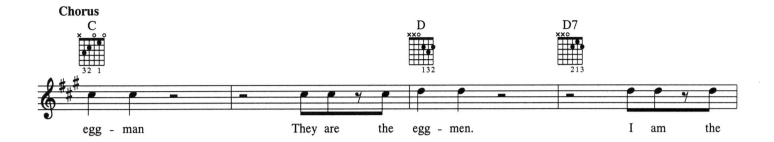

egg - man   They are   the   egg - men.   I   am   the

D.C. al Coda
(take Coda 2)

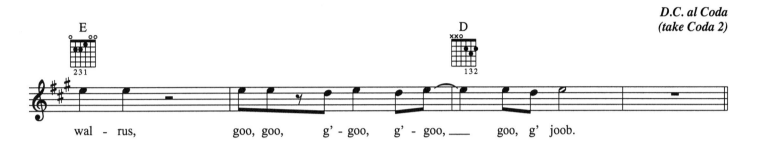

wal - rus,   goo, goo,   g' - goo, g' - goo, ___ goo, g' joob.

⊕ *Coda 2*

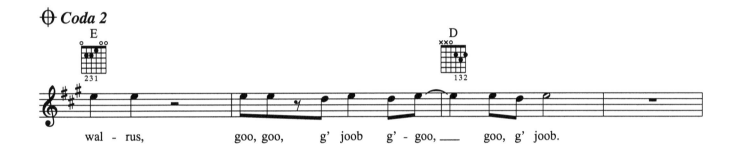

wal - rus,   goo, goo,   g' joob g' - goo, ___ goo, g' joob.

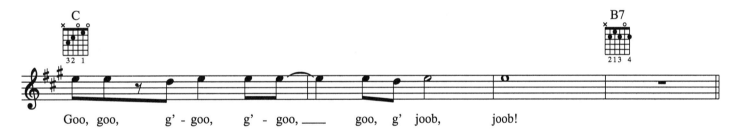

Goo, goo,   g' - goo,   g' - goo, ___   goo, g' joob,   joob!

Repeat and Fade

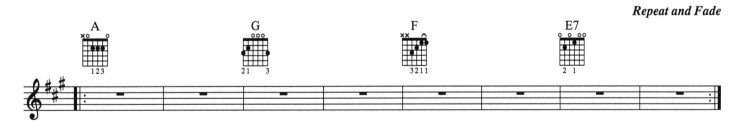

Additional Lyrics

3. Mister city p'liceman sitting pretty little p'licemen in a row.
   See how they fly like Lucy in the sky, see how they run.
   I'm crying.

5. Expert texpert choking smokers, don't you think the joker laughs at you?
   See how they smile, like pigs in a sty, see how they hide.
   I'm crying.

6. Semolina pilchards climbing up the Eiffel Tower.
   Element'ry penguin singing Hare Krishna.
   Man, you should have seen them kicking Edgar Allen Poe.

I Can See For Miles

Words and Music by Peter Townshend

Strum Pattern: 2
Pick Pattern: 1

Well here's a poke at you, __ you're gon-na choke on it too. __ You're gon-na

lose that smile _ be-cause all the while _____ I could see for miles and

miles. I could see for miles and miles. I can see for miles and miles and

miles and miles and miles. _____ Oh, yeah. _____

1.

2. **Interlude** *play 3 times* *D.S. al Coda*

4. I

✛ *Coda*
Verse

5. The Eif-fel Tower and the Taj Ma-hal are mine to see on clear days. __

You thought that I would need a crys-tal ball to see right through the haze. __

Well here's a poke at you, __ you're gon - na choke on it too. __ You're gon - na

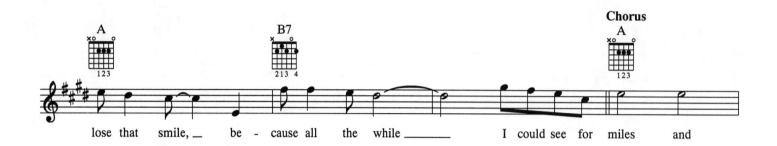

Chorus

lose that smile, __ be - cause all the while _____ I could see for miles and

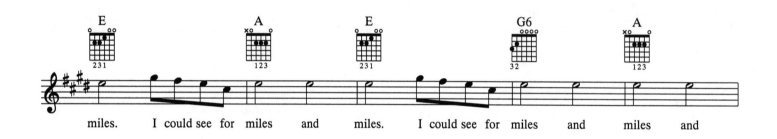

miles. I could see for miles and miles. I could see for miles and miles and

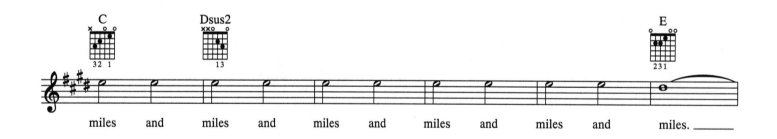

miles and miles and miles and miles and miles and miles. _____

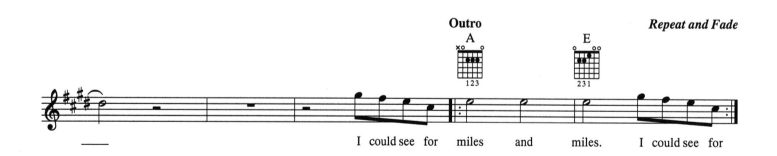

Outro   *Repeat and Fade*

_____ I could see for miles and miles. I could see for

Additional Lyrics

3. You took advantage of my trust in you when I was so far away.
I saw you holding lots of other guys, and now you have the nerve to say
That you still want me. Well, that's as maybe,
But you gotta stand trial, because all the while,

It's Only Rock 'N' Roll (But I Like It)

Words and Music by Mick Jagger and Keith Richards

Strum Pattern: 2
Pick Pattern: 3

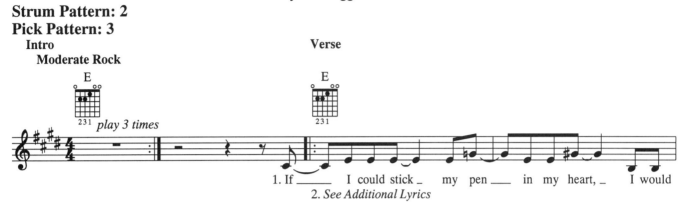

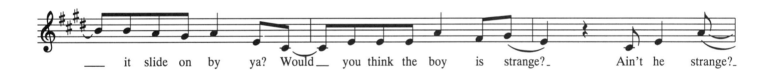

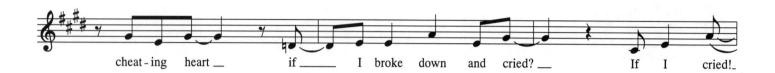

cheat - ing heart ___ if ___ I broke down and cried? ___ If I cried! ___

Chorus

___ I said, "I know ___ it's on - ly rock 'n' roll but I

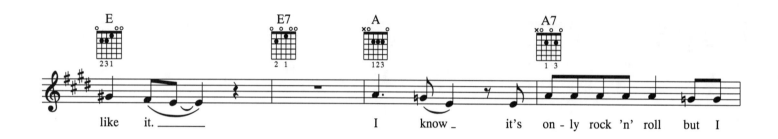

like it. ___ I know ___ it's on - ly rock 'n' roll but I

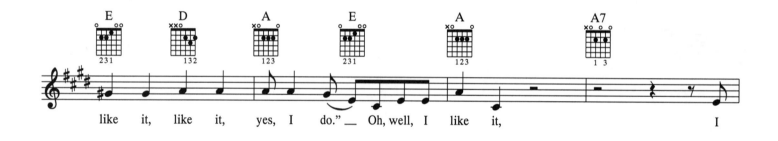

like it, like it, yes, I do." ___ Oh, well, I like it, I

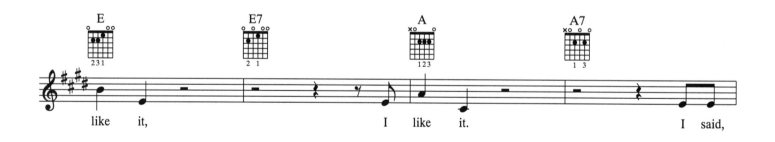

like it, I like it. I said,

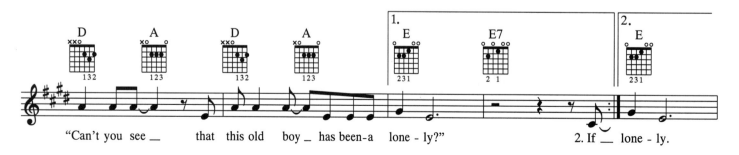

"Can't you see ___ that this old boy ___ has been-a lone - ly?" 2. If ___ lone - ly.

Bridge

And do ya think that you're the on-ly girl a - round? _____

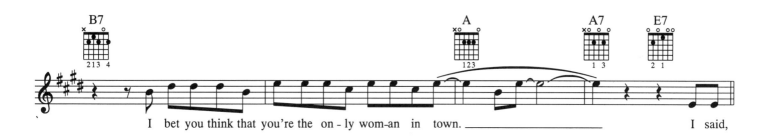

I bet you think that you're the on-ly wom-an in town. _____ I said,

Chorus

play 3 times

"I know _ it's on-ly rock 'n' roll but I like it. _____

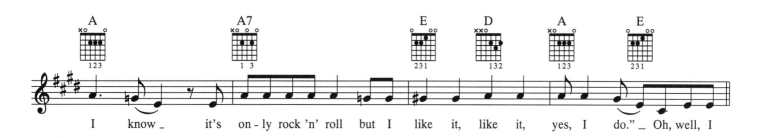

I know _ it's on-ly rock 'n' roll but I like it, like it, yes, I do." _ Oh, well, I

Outro

Repeat and Fade

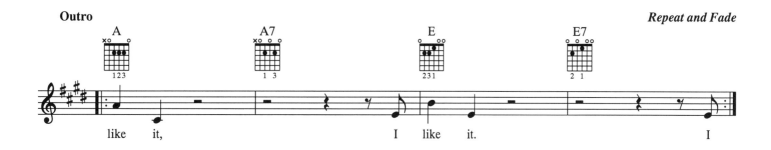

like it, I like it. I

Additional Lyrics

2. If I could stick a knife in my heart,
   Suicide right on the stage,
   Would it be enough for your teenage lust?
   Would it help to ease the pain?
   Ease your brain.
   If I could dig down deep in my heart,
   Feelings would flood on the page.
   Would it satisfy ya? Would it slide on by ya?
   Would ya think the boy's insane?
   He's insane.

I Love Rock 'N Roll

Words and Music by Alan Merrill and Jake Hooker

Additional Lyrics

2. He smiled, so I got up and asked him for his name.
"That don't matter," he said, "'cause it's all the same."
I said, "Can I take you home
Where we can be alone?"
And next we were moving on
And he was with me, yeah, me.
And next we were moving on.
And he was with me, yeah, me, singin';

3. I saw him dancing there by the record machine.
I knew he must have been about seventeen.
The beat was going strong,
Playing my fav'rite song,
And I could tell it wouldn't be long
'Til he was with me, yeah, me
And we'll be movin' on and singin' that same old song,
Yeah with me, singin';

Iron Man

Words and Music by Frank Iommi, John Osbourne, William Ward and Terence Butler

Strum Pattern: 1

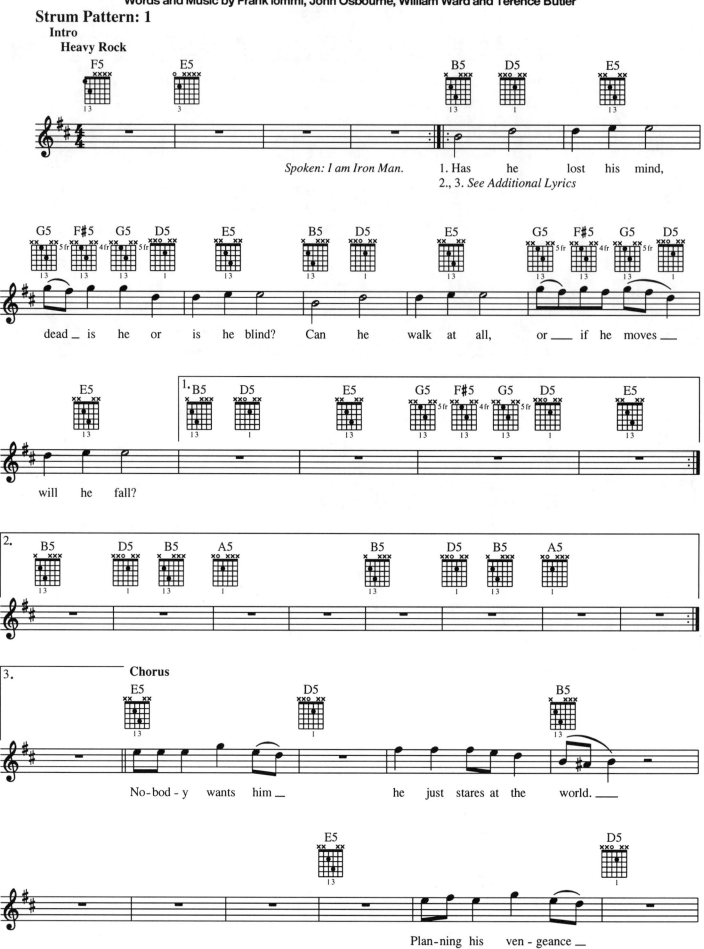

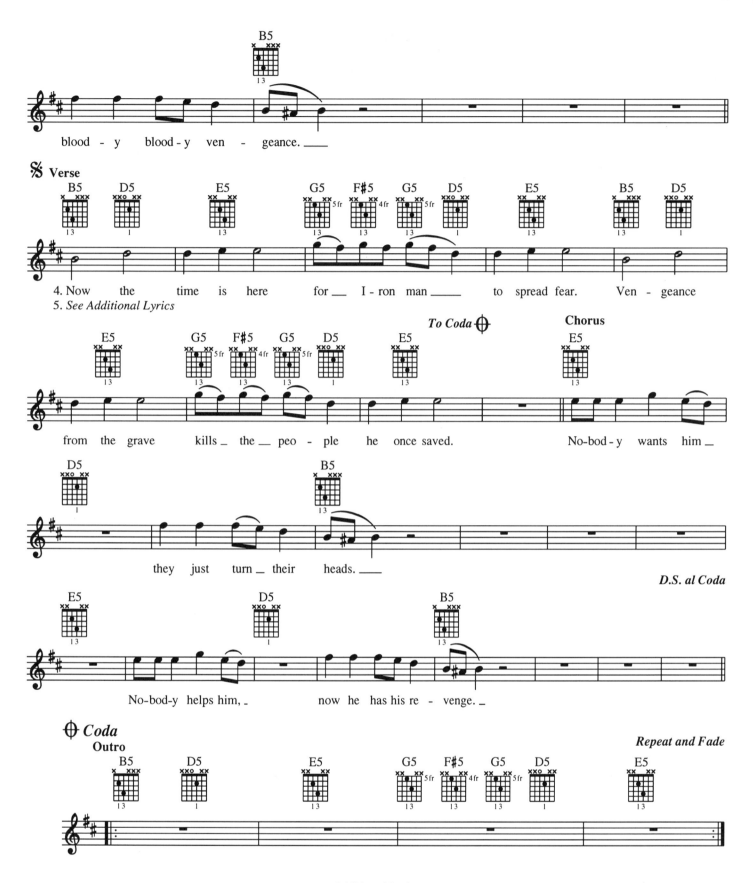

blood - y blood - y ven - geance. ____

Verse

4. Now the time is here for ___ I - ron man ____ to spread fear. Ven - geance
5. See Additional Lyrics

To Coda

Chorus

from the grave kills _ the _ peo - ple he once saved. No-bod - y wants him _

they just turn _ their heads. ____

D.S. al Coda

No-bod-y helps him, _ now he has his re - venge. _

Coda
Outro

Repeat and Fade

Additional Lyrics

2. Is he live or dead?
   Is his thoughts within his head?
   Wheel just passing there,
   Why should we even care?

3. He was turned to steel
   In the great magnetic field,
   When he traveled time
   For the future of mankind.

5. Heavy boots of lead
   Fills his victims full of lead,
   Running as fast as they can
   Iron man lives again.

Lady Madonna

Words and Music by John Lennon and Paul McCartney

Strum Pattern: 1
Pick Pattern: 1

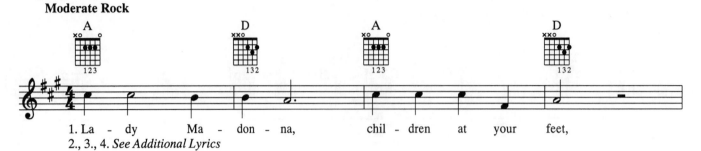

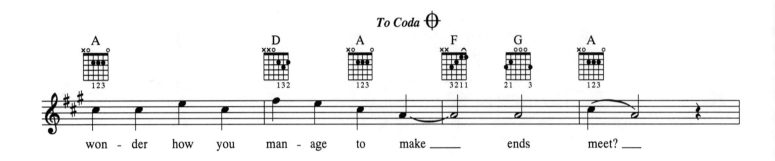

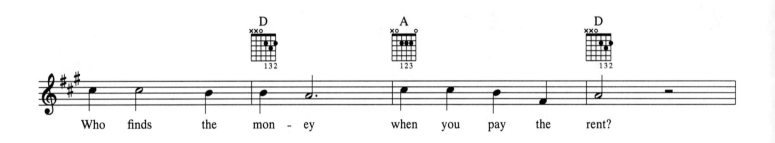

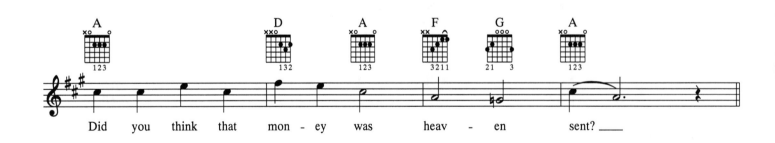

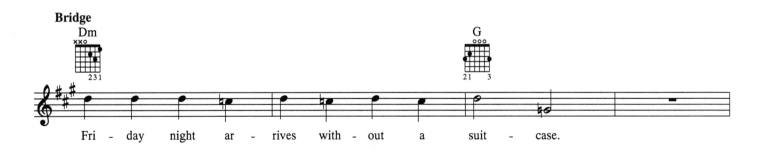

Additional Lyrics

2. Lady Madonna, baby at your breast,
   Wonder how you manage to feed the rest?
   (Instrumental to Chorus)

3. Lady Madonna, lying on the bed,
   Listen to the music playing in your head.
   (Instrumental to Bridge)

Bridge Tuesday afternoon is never ending;
         Wedn'sday morning papers didn't come.
         Thursday night your stockings needed mending.
         See how they run.

4. Lady Madonna, children at your feet,
   Wonder how you manage to make ends meet?

Lay Down Sally

Words and Music by Eric Clapton, Marcy Levy and George Terry

Strum Pattern: 1
Pick Pattern: 1

Verse
Bright Rock

1. There is noth-ing that is wrong _ in want-ing you to stay here with
2., 3. *See Additonal Lyrics*

me. I know you've got some-where to go, ___ but

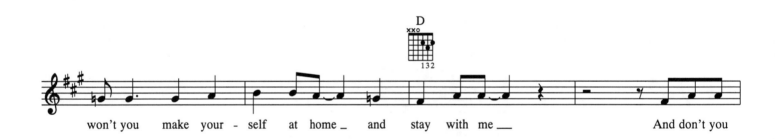

won't you make your-self at home _ and stay with me ___ And don't you

Chorus

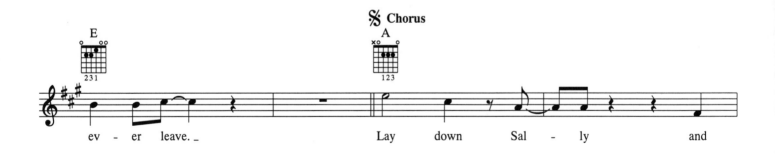

ev-er leave. _ Lay down Sal-ly and

rest here in ___ my arms. Don't you think you want _ some-one to talk _

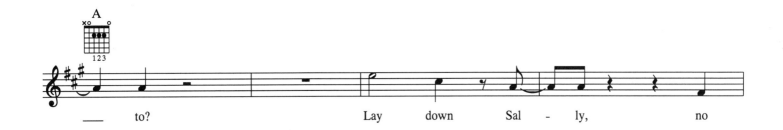

_to?_ Lay down Sal - ly, no

need to leave _ so soon. I've been try - ing all ___ night long _ just to

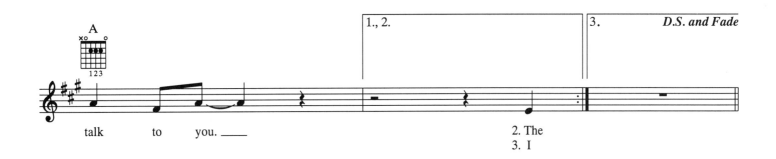

talk to you. ___

1., 2.

3.   *D.S. and Fade*

2. The
3. I

Additional Lyrics

2. The sun ain't nearly on the rise,
   And we still got the moon and stars above.
   Underneath the velvet skies, love is all that matters.
   Won't you stay with me?
   And don't you ever leave.

3. I long to see the morning light
   Coloring your face so dreamily.
   So don't you go and say goodbye,
   You can lay your worries down and stay with me.
   And don't you ever leave.

Layla

Words and Music by Eric Clapton and Jim Gordon

Strum Pattern: 4
Pick Pattern: 5

Verse
Moderate Rock

1. What will you do ____ when you get lone - ly? ____
2., 3. *See Additional Lyrics*

When no - bod - y's wait - ing by your side.

You've been run - ning and hid - ing much too long. ____

You know it's just ____ your fool - ish pride. Lay -

Chorus

la, _____ you got me on ____ my knees, Lay -

la, _____ I'm beg - ging dar - lin' please. Lay -

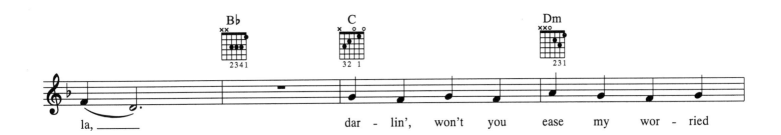

la, _____ dar - lin', won't you ease my wor - ried

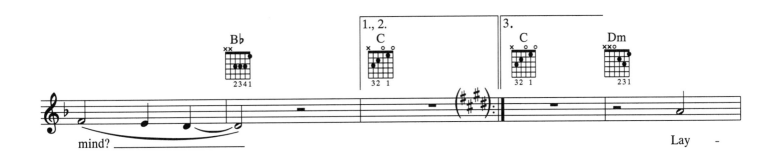

mind? _____ Lay -

Outro

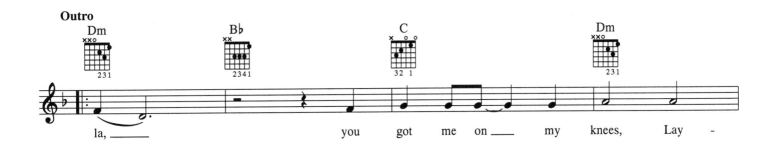

la, _____ you got me on ___ my knees, Lay -

Repeat and Fade

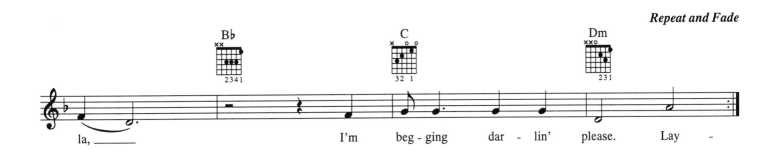

la, _____ I'm beg - ging dar - lin' please. Lay -

Additional Lyrics

2. Tried to give you consolation.
   Your old man won't let you down.
   Like a fool I fell in love with you,
   Turned the whole world upside down.

3. Let's make the best of the situation,
   Before I fin'ly go insane.
   Please don't say we'll never find a way,
   And tell me all my love's in vain.

Let It Ride

Words and Music by Randy Bachman and Charles Turner

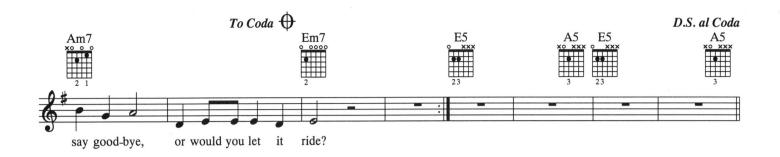

say good-bye,   or would you let   it   ride?

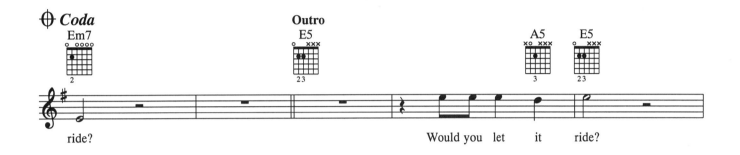

ride?   Would you let   it   ride?

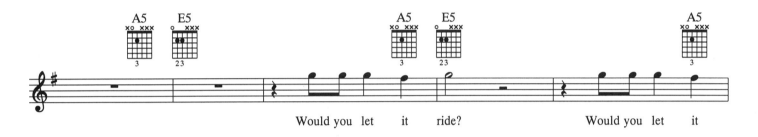

                    Would you let   it   ride?   Would you let   it

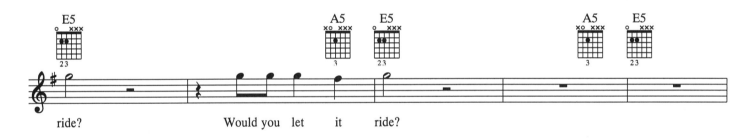

ride?   Would you let   it   ride?

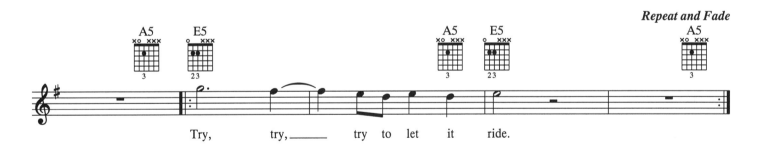

Try,   try,_____ try to let   it   ride.

Additional Lyrics

2. Well, my life is not complete.
   I never see you smile.
   Try, try, try to let it ride.
   Baby, you want the forgiving kind,
   And that's just not my style.
   Try, try, try to let it ride.

3. I've been doing things worth while,
   And you've been doin' time.
   Try, try, try to let it ride.

Lick It Up

Words and Music by Paul Stanley and Vincent Cusano

Strum Pattern: 1

Verse
Moderate Rock

1. Don't wan-na wait 'til you know me bet-ter.
2. *See Additional Lyrics*

Let's just be glad for the time to - geth - er.

Pre-Chorus

Life's such a treat and it's time you taste it.

There ain't no rea - son on earth to waste it. It ain't a crime to be good to your - self.

Chorus

Lick it up. Lick it up. Ah, ah, ah. It's on - ly right __ now.

Lick it up. Lick it up. Ah, ah, ah. Oo yeah.

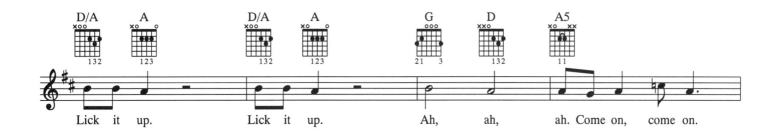

Lick it up. Lick it up. Ah, ah, ah. Come on, come on.

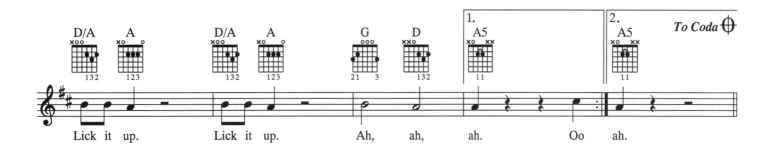

Lick it up. Lick it up. Ah, ah, ah. Oo ah.

Bridge

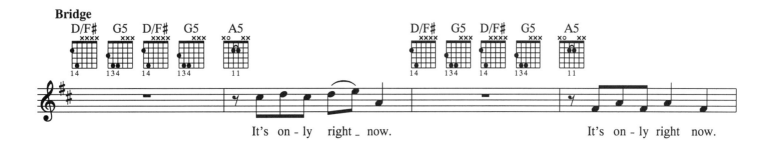

It's on - ly right _ now. It's on - ly right now.

D.S. al Coda
(take 2nd ending)

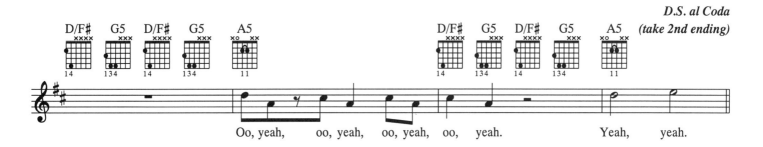

Oo, yeah, oo, yeah, oo, yeah, oo, yeah. Yeah, yeah.

⊕ *Coda*
Outro

Repeat and Fade

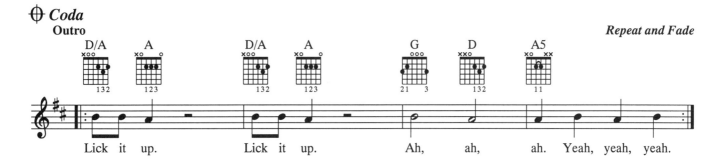

Lick it up. Lick it up. Ah, ah, ah. Yeah, yeah, yeah.

Additional Lyrics

2. Don't need to wait for an invitation.
You gotta live like you're on vacation.
There's something sweet you can't buy with money.
Lick it up. Whoa. Lick it up.
It's all you need, so believe me honey.
It ain't a crime to be good to yourself.

Let It Be

Words and Music by John Lennon and Paul McCartney

Strum Pattern: 5
Pick Pattern: 6

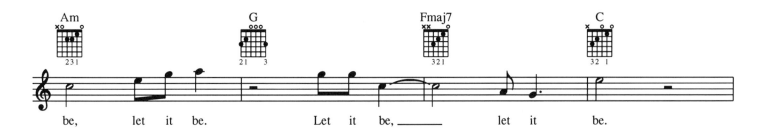

be,   let it be.   Let it be, _____ let it be.

To Coda ⊕   *D.S. al Coda*

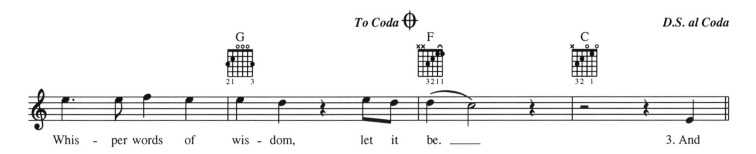

Whis - per words of wis - dom,   let it be. _____   3. And

⊕ **Coda**   **Outro**

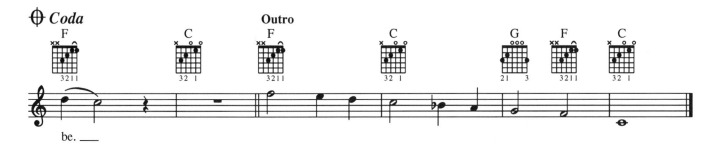

be. ___

Additional Lyrics

2. And when the broken hearted people
Living in the world agree,
There will be an answer, let it be.
For tho' they may be parted
There is still a chance that they will see,
There will be an answer, let it be.

3. And when the night is cloudy
There is still a light that shines on me,
Shine until tomorrow, let it be.
I wake up to the sound of music
Mother Mary comes to me,
Speaking words of wisdom, let it be.

Love Me Do

Words and Music by John Lennon and Paul McCartney

Strum Pattern: 5
Pick Pattern: 3

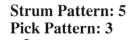

Intro
Moderate Rock

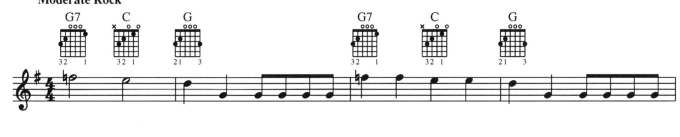

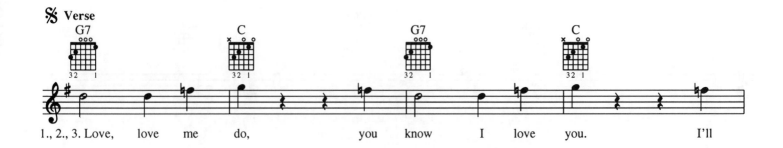

Verse

1., 2., 3. Love, love me do, you know I love you. I'll

al - ways be true, so please. _____ love me

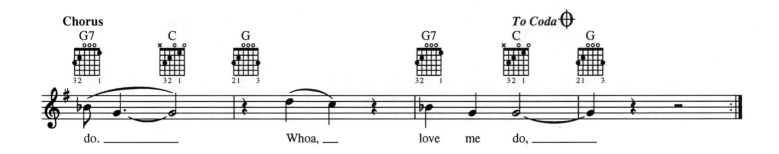

Chorus   *To Coda* ✛

do. _____ Whoa, ___ love me do, _____

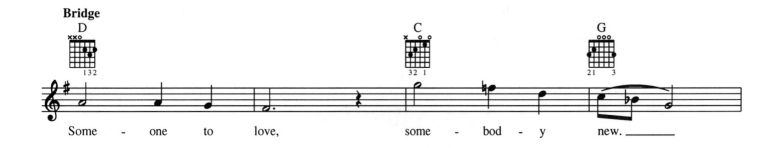

Bridge

Some - one to love, some - bod - y new. _____

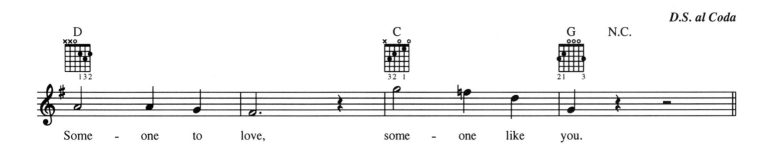

D.S. al Coda

Some - one to love, some - one like you.

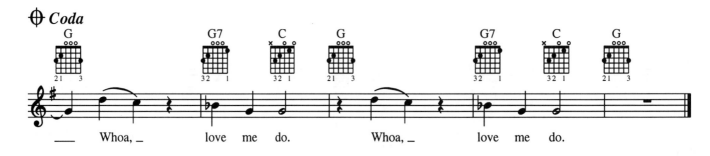

✛ *Coda*

___ Whoa, _ love me do. Whoa, _ love me do.

Mr. Crowley

Words and Music by Ozzy Osbourne, Randy Rhoads and Bob Daisley

Strum Pattern: 2
Pick Pattern: 4

Verse
Moderate Heavy Rock

1. Mis - ter Crow-ley, what went on in your head? Oh, Mis - ter
2., 3. *See Additional Lyrics*

Crow-ley, did you talk with the dead? Your life-style to me seemed so

trag-ic. With the thrill of it all you fooled all the peo - ple with mag-ic. Yeah, you

wait-ed on Sa-tan's call 2. Mis - ter wall. Was it po-lem-i-c'lly sent?

I wan-na know what you meant. I wan-na know, I wan-na know what you meant. Yeah.

Additional Lyrics

2. Mister Charming,
   Did you think you were pure?
   Mister Alarming,
   In nocturning rapport.
   Uncovering things that were sacred,
   Manifest on this earth.
   Ah, conceived in the eye of a secret
   And they scattered the afterbirth.

3. Mister Crowley,
   Won't you ride my white horse?
   Mister Crowley,
   It's symbolic, of course.
   Approaching a time that is classic,
   I hear the maidens call.
   Approaching a time that is drastic,
   Standing with their backs to the wall.

Maggie May

Words and Music by Rod Stewart and Martin Quittenton

Strum Pattern: 2
Pick Pattern: 6

Intro

Medium Rock beat

Verse

1. Wake up, Mag-gie, I think I got some-thing to say to you.   It's
2., 3., 4. *See Additional Lyrics*

late Sep-tem-ber and I real-ly should ___ be back at ___ school.

I know I keep you a-mused,   but I

feel I'm be-ing used.   Oh, Mag-gie, I could-n't have

tried ___   an-y more. ___   You

led me a-way from home just to save you from be-ing a-

lone. You stole my heart, ___ and that's what real-ly

1., 2., 3.

4.

hurts.

2. The

Outro

Repeat and Fade

Additional Lyrics

2. The morning sun, when it's in your face,
   Really shows your age.
   But that don't worry me none.
   In my eyes, you're everything.
   I laughed at all of your jokes.
   My love you didn't need to coax.
   Oh, Maggie, I couldn't have tried any more.
   You let me away from home
   Just to save you from being alone.
   You stole my soul, and that's a pain I can do without.

3. All I needed was a friend
   To lend a guiding hand.
   But you turned into a lover, and, mother, what a lover!
   You wore me out.
   All you did was wreck my bed,
   And, in the morning, kick me in the head.
   Oh, Maggie, I couldn't have tried any more.
   You led me away from home
   'Cause you didn't want to be alone.
   You stole my heart, I couldn't leave you if I tried.

4. I suppose I could collect my books
   And get on back to school.
   Or steal my daddy's cue
   And make a living out of playing pool.
   Or find myself a rock 'n' roll band
   That needs a helping hand.
   Oh, Maggie, I wish I'd never seen your face.
   You made a first-class fool out of me.
   But I'm as blind as a fool can be.
   You stole my heart, but I love you anyway.

The Magic Bus

Words and Music by Peter Townshend

Strum Pattern: 2
Pick Pattern: 1

Verse
Bright Rock

1. Ev – 'ry - day __ I get in the queue. _ Too much, the ma-gic bus! _ To
2., 4., 5. *See Additional Lyrics*

get on the bus that takes me to you. Too much, the ma - gic bus! _

I'm so ner - vous, I ____ just sit and smile. _ Your

house is on - ly an - oth - er mile. _ Too much, the ma - gic bus! _

Interlude

Verse

3. I don't care how
6. *See Additional Lyrics*

much I pay. Too much, the ma - gic bus! _ Drive my bus to my

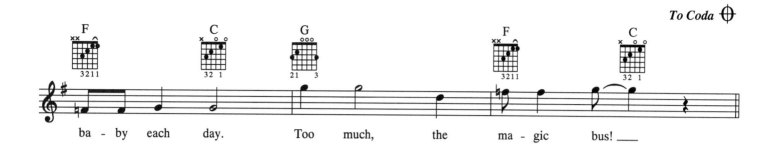

ba - by each day. Too much, the ma - gic bus! ___

Chorus

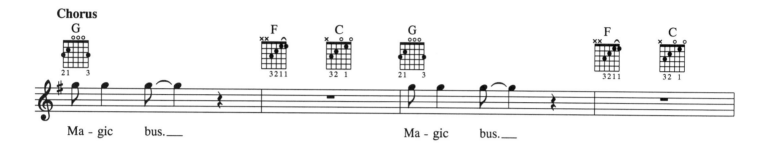

Ma - gic bus.___ Ma - gic bus.___

D.C. al Coda
(take repeat)

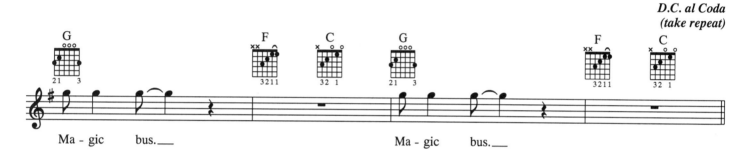

Ma - gic bus.___ Ma - gic bus.___

⊕ *Coda*
Outro

Repeat and Fade

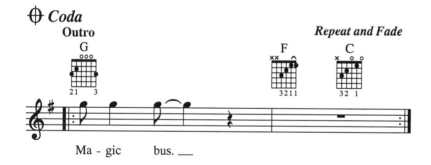

Ma - gic bus. ___

Additional Lyrics

2. Thank you, driver, for gettin' me here.
   You'll be an inspector, have no fear.
   I don't wanna cause no fuss,
   But can I buy your magic bus?

4. Three pence and six pence everyday,
   Just to drive to my baby.
   Three pence and six pence each day;
   Drive my baby every way.

5. Now I got my magic bus.
   I said, "Now I got my magic bus."
   I drive my baby every way.
   Each time I go a different way.

6 Everyday you'll see the dust,
   I drive my baby in the magic bus.

Magic Carpet Ride

Words and Music by John Kay and Rushton Moreve

Strum Pattern: 6
Pick Pattern: 6
Verse
Moderate Rock

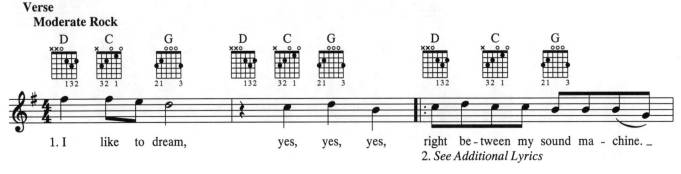

1. I like to dream, yes, yes, yes, right be-tween my sound ma-chine. _
2. *See Additional Lyrics*

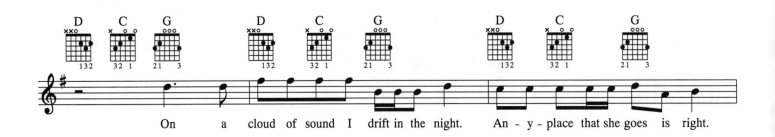

On a cloud of sound I drift in the night. An-y-place that she goes is right.

𝄋 Chorus

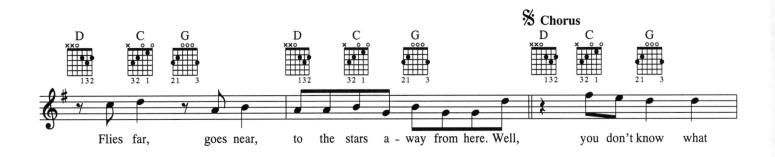

Flies far, goes near, to the stars a-way from here. Well, you don't know what

we can find. Oh, why don't you come with me, lit-tle girl, on a ma-gic car-pet ride?

MCA music publishing

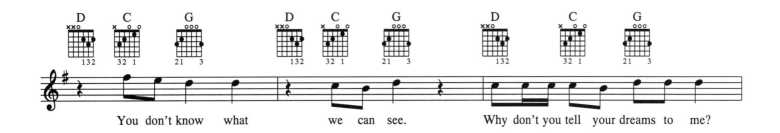

You don't know what we can see. Why don't you tell your dreams to me?

Fan - ta - sy will set you free. Close your eyes, girl. Look in - side, girl.

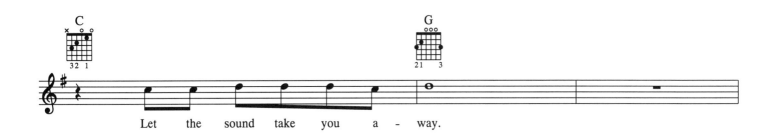

Let the sound take you a - way.

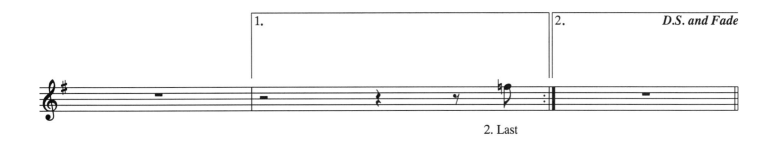

1.

2.   *D.S. and Fade*

2. Last

Additional Lyrics

2. Last night I found Aladdin's lamp,
And so I wished that I could stay,
Before the thing could answer me,
Well, someone came and took the lamp away.
I looked around.
A lousy candle's all I found.

Mississippi Queen

Words and Music by Leslie West, Felix Pappalardi, Corky Laing and D. Rea

Strum Pattern: 1

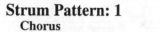

Mis - sis - sip - pi Queen,_____ do you

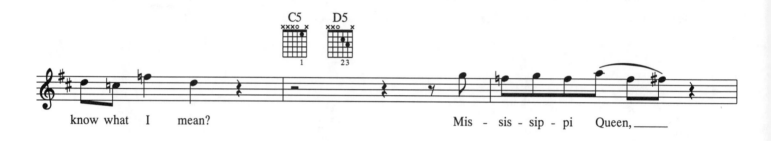

know what I mean? Mis - sis - sip - pi Queen,_____

she taught me ev - 'ry - thing.

1. Way
2. *See Additional Lyrics*

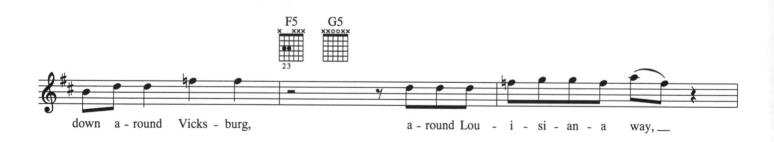

down a - round Vicks - burg, a - round Lou - i - si - an - a way,_____

lived a Ca - jun la - dy called the

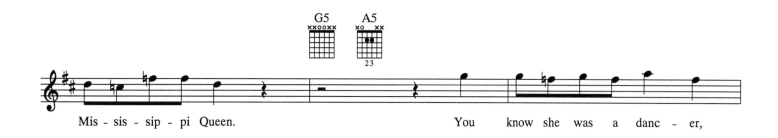

Mis - sis - sip - pi Queen. You know she was a danc - er,

she moved bet - ter on wine. While the rest of them dudes was a

To Coda *D.C. al Coda*

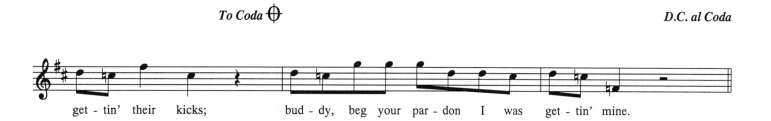

get - tin' their kicks; bud - dy, beg your par - don I was get - tin' mine.

 Coda

broth-er, beg your par-don I was get-tin' mine. __ Hey, _____ Mis-sis-sip-pi Queen. __

Additional Lyrics

2. This lady she asked me
   If I would be her man.
   You know that I told her
   I'd do what I can
   To keep her lookin' pretty.
   Buy her dresses that shine.
   While the rest of them dudes was a-makin' their bread;
   Buddy, beg your pardon I was losin' mine.

More Than A Feeling

Words and Music by Tom Scholz

Strum Pattern: 3, 4
Pick Pattern: 3

1. I looked out this morn-ing and the sun was gone,
2. *See Additional Lyrics*

turned on some mu - sic to start my day, then lost my - self in a fa -

mil - iar song. I closed my eyes and I slipped a - way.

It's more than a feel - ing when I

hear that old song they used to play. And I be - gin dream - in'

till I see Mar - y Ann walk a - way. I see my

Additional Lyrics

2. So many people have come and gone,
   Their faces fade as the years go by.
   Yet I still recall as I wonder on,
   As clear as the sun in the summer sky.

My Generation

Words and Music by Peter Townshend

Strum Pattern: 4
Pick Pattern: 5

Verse
Fast Rock

1. Peo - ple try to put us down. Talk - in' 'bout my gen - er - a - tion.
2., 3. *See Additional Lyrics*

Just be-cause we get a - round. Talk - in' 'bout my gen - er - a - tion.

Things they do look aw - ful cold. Talk - in' 'bout my gen - er - a - tion.

Hope I die be - fore I get old. This is my gen - er -

Chorus

a - tion. ___ This is my gen-er - a - tion, ba - by. ___

Additional Lyrics

2., 3. Why don't you all fade away? Talkin' 'bout my generation.
Don't try to dig what we all say. Talkin' 'bout my generation.
I'm not tryin' to cause a big sensation. Talkin' 'bout my generation.
I'm just talkin' 'bout my generation. Talkin' 'bout my generation.

Nights In White Satin

Words and Music by Justin Hayward

*Strum Pattern: 9
*Pick Pattern: 8

Verse
Slow Ballad

1. Nights in white sat - in, _____ nev-er reach-ing the end. Let-ters I've
2. *See Additional Lyrics*

*play 2 times per meas.

writ - ten, _____ nev-er mean-ing to send. Beau-ty I'd al-ways missed

with these eyes _ be - fore. Just what the truth is _____ I can't say an-y-

Chorus

more. _____ 'Cause I love you. _____ Yes, I __ love you. _____ Oh, _____ how I

1. love _ you. _____ 2. love _ you. _____

_____ Oh, _ how I love you. _____

Additional Lyrics

2. Gazing and people, some hand in hand,
Just what I'm going through, they can't understand.
Some try to tell me thoughts they can not defend,
Just what you want to be, you'll be in the end.
And I...

The Night They Drove Old Dixie Down

Words and Music by Robbie Robertson

Strum Pattern: 3
Pick Pattern: 3
Verse
Moderate Rock Ballad

1. Vir - gil Caine is the name __ and I served on the Dan - ville
2., 3. *See Additional Lyrics*

train __ 'til Stone - man's cav - al - ry came _ and tore up the tracks a -

gain. __ In the win - ter of 'six - ty - five, we were

hun - gry, just bare - ly a - live. __ By May the tenth,

Rich - mond had fell. __ It's a time __ I re - mem - ber, oh, so well: The

Chorus

night they drove old Dix - ie down, __ and the bells __ were ring - in'; the

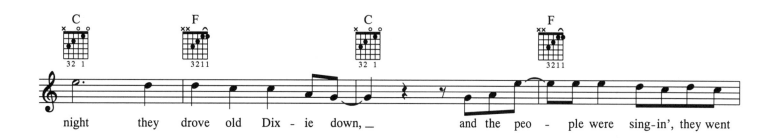

night they drove old Dix - ie down, __ and the peo - ple were sing-in', they went

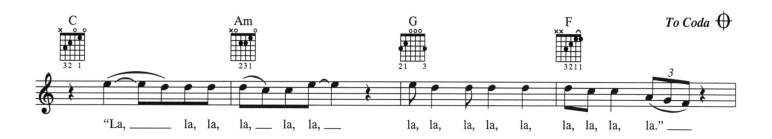

"La, _____ la, la, la, __ la, la, __ la, la, la, la, la, la, la, la, la." __

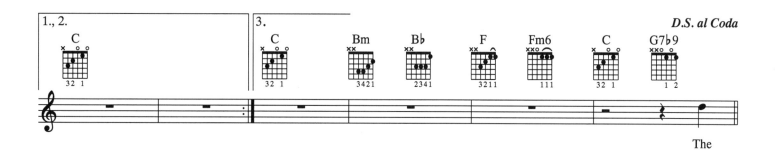

The

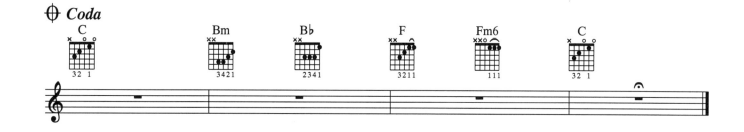

Additional Lyrics

2. Back with my wife in Tennessee,
   When one day she called to me,
   "Virgil, quick, come see,
   There goes Robert E. Lee."
   Now, I don't mind choppin' wood,
   And I don't care if the money's no good.
   Ya take what ya need and ya leave the rest,
   But they should never have taken the very best.

3. Like my father before me,
   I will work the land.
   And like my brother above me,
   Who took the Rebel stand;
   He was just eighteen, proud and brave,
   But a Yankee laid him in his grave.
   I swear by the mud below my feet,
   Ya can't raise a Caine back up when he's in defeat.

Oh! Darling

Words and Music by John Lennon and Paul McCartney

Strum Pattern: 1, 3
Pick Pattern: 2, 4

1. Oh __ dar-ling, please be-lieve me, _____ I'll nev-er do you no
2. See Additional Lyrics

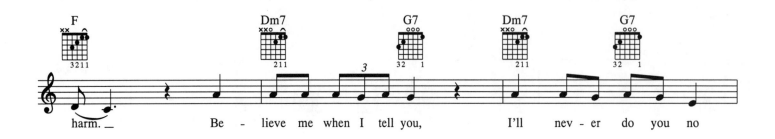

harm. __ Be - lieve me when I tell you, I'll nev-er do you no

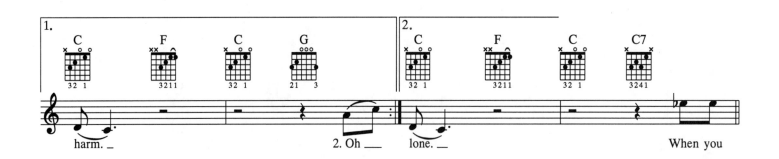

1. harm. __

2. Oh ___ lone. __ When you

Chorus

told me you did-n't need me an-y-more, well you know I near-ly broke down and

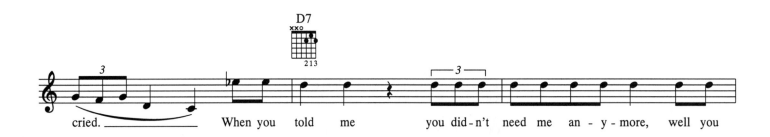

cried. _____ When you told me you did-n't need me an-y-more, well you

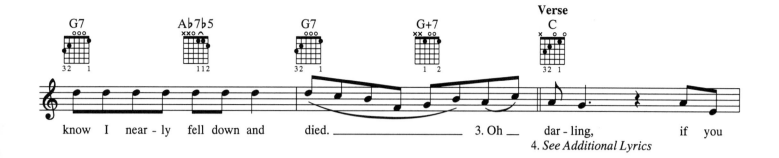

know I near-ly fell down and died. _____ 3. Oh __ dar-ling, if you
4. *See Additional Lyrics*

leave me, _____ I'll nev-er make it a lone. _____ Be -

lieve me when I tell you, I'll nev-er do you no harm. _ *Spoken: Believe me, darling.* When you

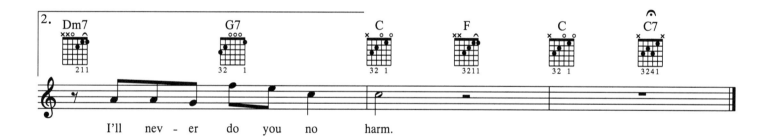

I'll nev-er do you no harm.

Additional Lyrics

2. Oh darling, if you leave me,
   I'll never make it alone.
   Believe me when I beg you,
   Don't ever leave me alone.

4. Oh, darling, please believe me,
   I'll never let you down.
   Believe me when I tell you,
   I'll never do you no harm.

Owner Of A Lonely Heart

Words and Music by Trevor Horn, Jon Anderson, Trevor Rabin and Chris Squire

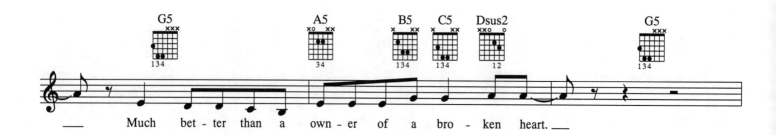

Much bet - ter than a own - er of a bro - ken heart. ___

Own - er of a lone - ly heart. ___

⊕ Coda

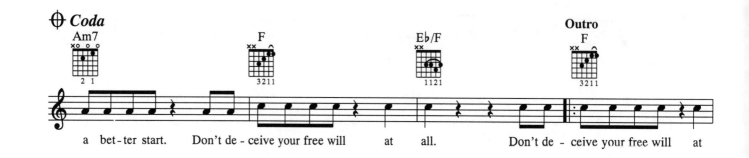

a bet - ter start. Don't de - ceive your free will at all. Don't de - ceive your free will at

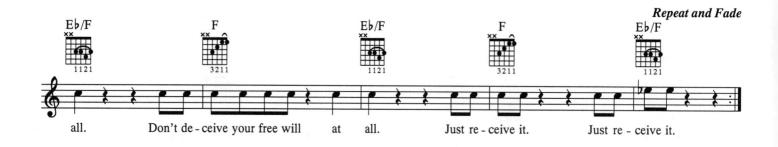

all. Don't de - ceive your free will at all. Just re - ceive it. Just re - ceive it.

Additional Lyrics

2. Say you don't want to change it.
You've been hurt so before.
Watch it now, the eagle in the sky,
How he's dancin' one and only.
You lose yourself.
No, not for pity's sake.
There's no real reason to be lonely.
Be yourself.
Give your free will a chance.
You've got to want to succeed.

4. Sooner or later each conclusion will decide the lonely heart.
It will excite it, will delight it,
Will give a better start.
Don't deceive your free will at all.

Rebel, Rebel

Words and Music by David Bowie

Strum Pattern: 1
Pick Pattern: 4
Intro
Moderate Rock

Do, do, do, do, ___ do, do, do, do.

Verse

1. Got your moth - er in a whirl. ___ She's not sure if you're a
2. *See Additional Lyrics*

boy or a girl. ___ Hey babe, ___ your hair's al - right. ___

Hey babe, let's go out to - night. ___ You like me and I

like it all. ___ We like danc - ing and we look di - vine. ___

You love bands when they play it hard. ___ You want more and you

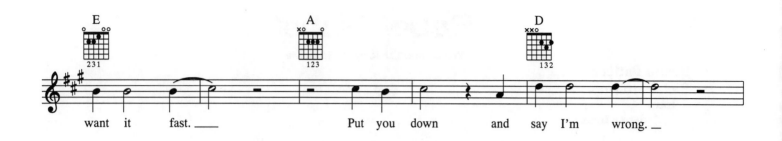

want it fast. _____ Put you down and say I'm wrong. _

%% Chorus

You tack-y thing, and put them on. _____ Reb-el, reb-el, you've

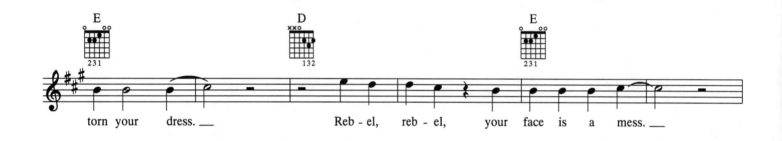

torn your dress. _ Reb-el, reb-el, your face is a mess. _

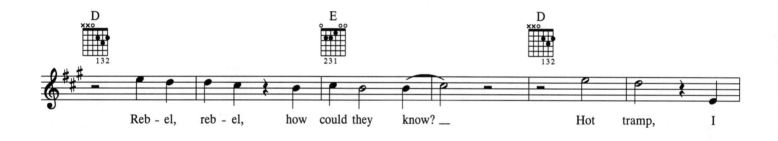

Reb-el, reb-el, how could they know? _ Hot tramp, I

To Coda ⊕

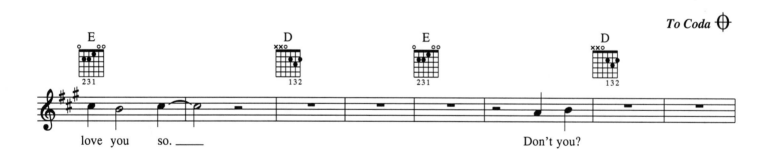

love you so. _____ Don't you?

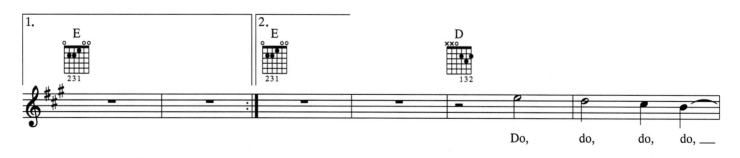

Do, do, do, do, _____

do, do, do, do. Do, do, do, do, ___ do, do, do, do.

⊕ Coda   **Outro**

3. You've torn your dress. __ Your face is a mess. __ You
4. *See Additional Lyrics*

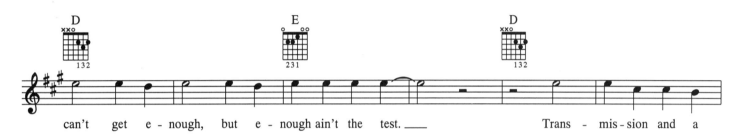

can't get e - nough, but e - nough ain't the test. ___ Trans - mis - sion and a

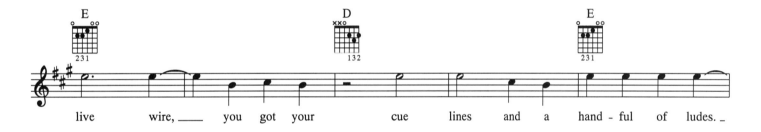

live wire, ___ you got your cue lines and a hand - ful of ludes. _

Repeat and Fade

__ You wan - na dan - ger when they count out the pews. __ 4. But you

Additional Lyrics

2. Got your mother in a whirl,
   'Cause she's not sure if you're a boy or a girl.
   Hey babe, your hair's alright.
   Hey babe, let's stay out tonight.

4. But you love your dress.
   You're a juvenile success,
   Because your face is a mess.
   So how could they know?
   I said, "How could they know?"

Reelin' In The Years

Words and Music by Walter Becker and Donald Fagen

Strum Pattern: 3
Pick Pattern: 3

Verse
Brisk Shuffle

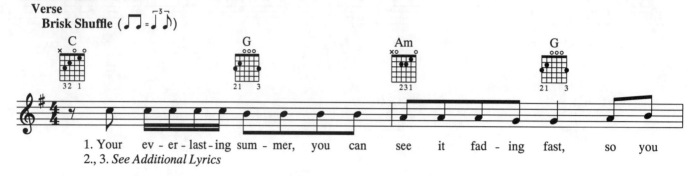

1. Your ev-er-last-ing sum-mer, you can see it fad-ing fast, so you
2., 3. See Additional Lyrics

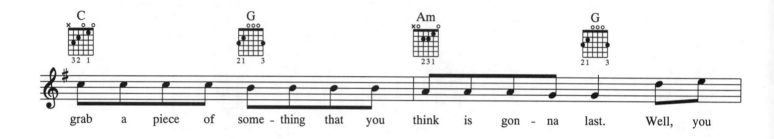

grab a piece of some-thing that you think is gon-na last. Well, you

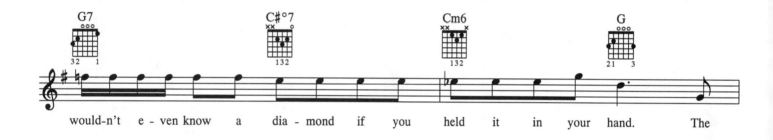

would-n't e-ven know a dia-mond if you held it in your hand. The

Chorus

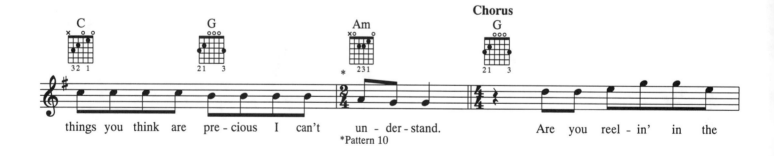

things you think are pre-cious I can't un-der-stand.   Are you reel-in' in the
*Pattern 10

years, ___   stow-in' a-way the time? ___   Are you gath-er-in' up the

MCA music publishing

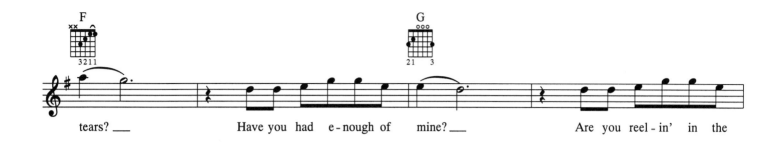

tears? ___   Have you had e-nough of   mine? ___   Are you reel-in' in the

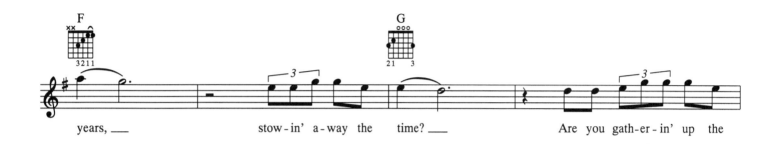

years, ___   stow-in' a-way the   time? ___   Are you gath-er-in' up the

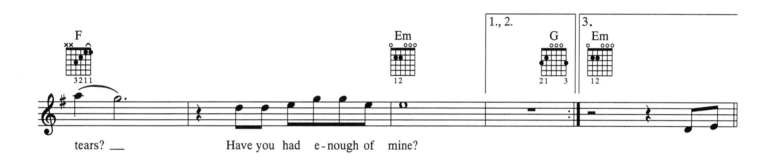

tears? ___   Have you had e-nough of   mine?

Outro   *Repeat and Fade*

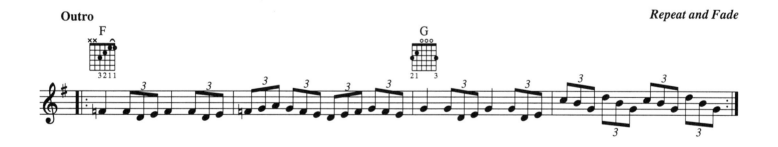

Additional Lyrics

2. You've been tellin' me you're a genius since you were seventeen.
   In all the time I've known you I still don't know what you mean.
   The weekend at the college didn't turn out like you planned.
   The things you pass for knowledge I can't understand.

3. I've spent a lot of money and I've spent a lot of time.
   The trip we made to Hollywood is etched upon my mind.
   After all the things we've done and seen, you find another man.
   The things you think are useless I can't understand.

Revolution

Words and Music by John Lennon and Paul McCartney

Strum Pattern: 2
Pick Pattern: 2

Verse
Moderate Shuffle

1. You say you want a rev-o - lu - tion, ___ well ___ you know, ___ we all want to change the
2., 3. *See Additional Lyrics*

*Use strum & pick patterns 10 for all 2/4 meas.

world. You tell me that it's e-vo - lu - tion, ___ well ___ you know, ___ we all want to change the

world. ___ But when you talk a-bout de-struc-tion, ___ don't you know that you can count me out.

Chorus

Don't you know it's gon-na be al - right, al - right, al - right.

1., 2.

3.

Outro

play 3 times

2. You Al - right, al - right, al - right, al -right.

Additional Lyrics

2. You say you got a real solution,
Well you know,
We'd all love to see the plan.
You ask me for a contribution,
Well you know,
We're all doing what we can.
But if you want money for people with minds that hate,
All I can tell you is, "Brother you have to wait."

3. You say you'll change the constitution,
Well you know,
We all want to change your head.
You tell me it's the institution,
Well you know,
You better free your mind instead.
But if you go carrying pictures of Chairman Mao,
You ain't going to make it with anyone, anyhow.

Rock On

Words and Music by David Essex

Strum Pattern: 3
Pick Pattern: 1

Rock And Roll All Nite

Words and Music by Paul Stanley and Gene Simmons

Strum Pattern: 1
Pick Pattern: 1

Verse

Moderate Rock

1. You show us ev - 'ry - thing you got. ___ You keep on danc - in' and the
2. *See Additional Lyrics*

room ___ gets hot. You drive us wild, we'll drive you cra - zy.

You say you want to go for a spin. The par - ty's just be - gun; we'll

let you in. You drive us wild, we'll drive you cra - zy.

Pre-Chorus

You keep on shout - in'. You keep on shout - in'.

Chorus

I ___ wan - na rock 'n' roll all night ___

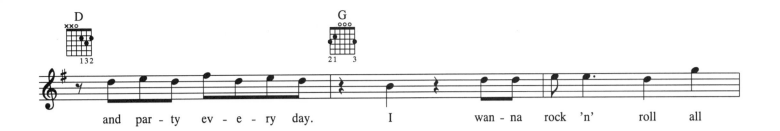

and par - ty ev - e - ry day.   I   wan - na   rock 'n'   roll   all

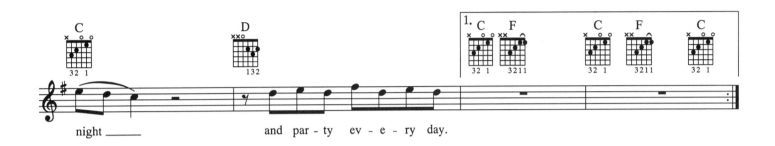

night _____   and par - ty   ev - e - ry   day.

2.

I   wan - na   rock 'n'   roll   all   night _____   and par - ty   ev - e - ry   day.

I   wan - na   rock 'n'   roll   all   night _____   and par - ty   ev - e - ry   day.

Outro   *Play 6 Times and Fade*

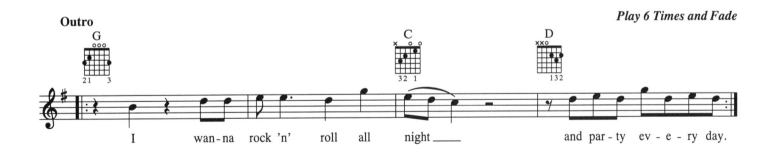

I   wan - na   rock 'n'   roll   all   night _____   and par - ty   ev - e - ry   day.

Additional Lyrics

2. You keep on sayin' you'll be mine for a while,
     You're lookin' fancy and I like your style.
     You drive us wild, and we'll drive you crazy.
     You show us everything you got.
     Baby, baby that's quite a lot.
     You drive us wild, we'll drive you crazy.
     You keep on shoutin'. You keep on shoutin'.

Rock And Roll Hoochie Koo

Words and Music by Rick Derringer

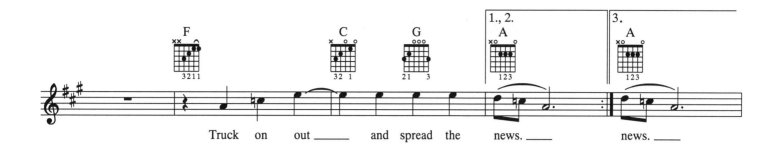

Truck on out ____ and spread the news. ____ news. ____

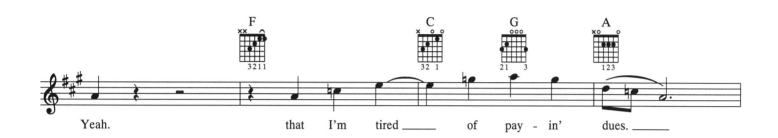

Yeah. that I'm tired ____ of pay - in' dues. ____

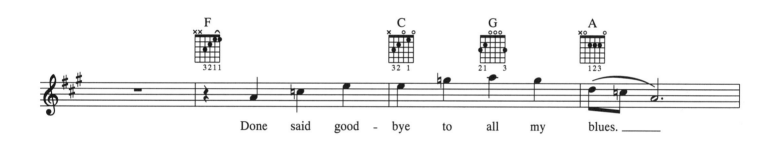

Done said good - bye to all my blues. ____

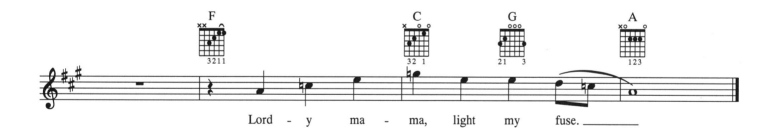

Lord - y ma - ma, light my fuse. ____

Additional Lyrics

2. Mosquitos started buzzing 'bout this time of year.
Going out back she said she'll meet me there.
We were rolling in the grass that grows behind the barn.
You know my ears started ringing like a fire alarm.

3. I hope you all know what I'm talkin' about.
The way they wiggle that thing really knocks me out.
Gettin' higher all the time hope you all are too.
C'mon a little closer gonna do it to you.

Rock The Casbah

Words and Music by The Clash

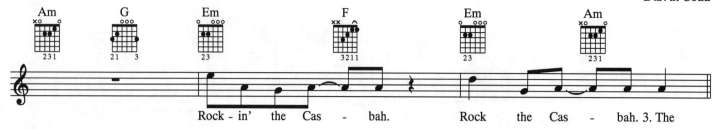

Rock - in' the Cas - bah. Rock the Cas - bah. 3. The

⊕ *Coda*

Outro

Rock the Cas - bah, Sha - rif _____ don't like it. ____

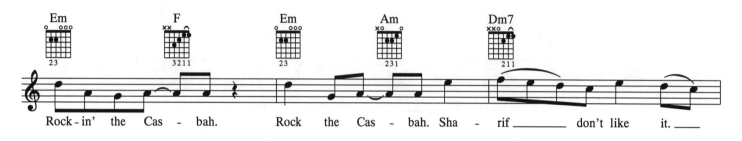

Rock - in' the Cas - bah. Rock the Cas - bah. Sha - rif _____ don't like it. ____

Repeat and Fade

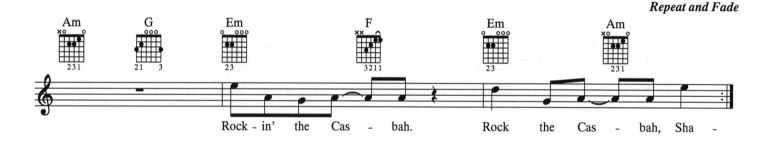

Rock - in' the Cas - bah. Rock the Cas - bah, Sha -

Additional Lyrics

2. By order of the prophet,
   We ban that boogie sound.
   Degenerate the faithful
   With that crazy Casbah sound.
   But the Bedouin, they brought out
   The electric camel drum.
   The local guitar picker
   Got his guitar picking thumb.
   As soon as the Sharif had cleared the square,
   They began to wail.

3. The king called up his jet fighters,
   He said, "You better earn your pay.
   Drop your bombs between the minarets
   Down the Casbah way."
   As soon as the Sharif
   Was chauffeured outta there,
   The jet pilots tuned
   To the cockpit radio blare.
   As soon as a Sharif was outta their hair,
   The jet pilots wailed.

Rocky Mountain Way

Words and Music by Joe Walsh, Joe Vitale, Ken Passarelli and Rocke Grace

Strum Pattern: 1
Pick Pattern: 1

Additional Lyrics

2. Well, he's tellin' us this and he's tellin' us that,
   Changes it every day;
   Says it doesn't matter.
   Bases are loaded and Casey's at bat,
   Playin' it play by play;
   Time to change the batter.

Roxanne

Words and Music by Sting

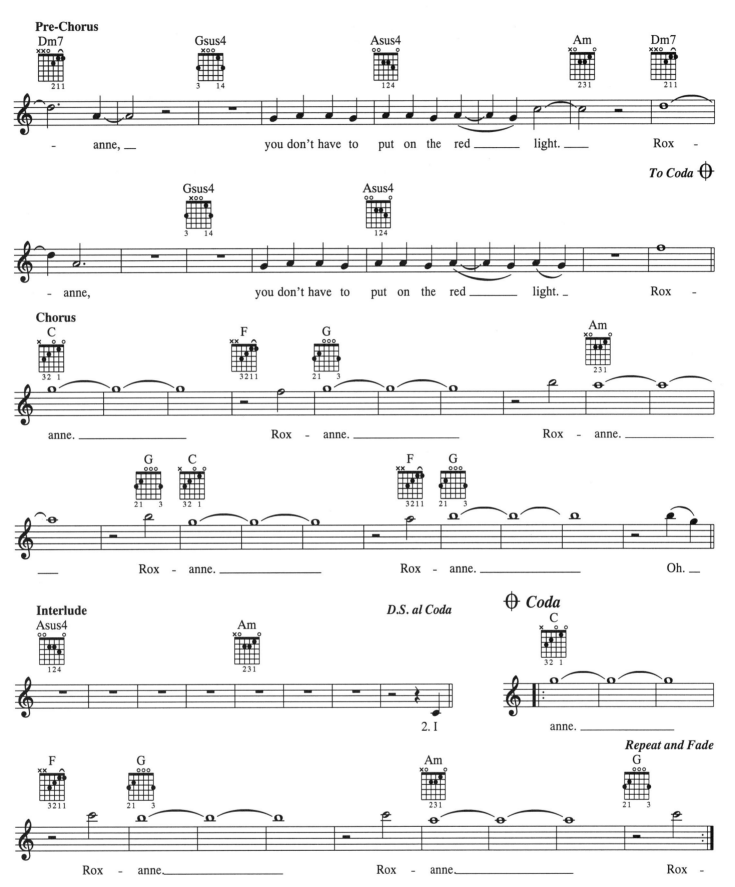

Additional Lyrics

2. I loved you since I knew ya.
   I wouldn't talk down to ya.
   I have to tell you just how I feel.
   I won't share you with another boy.
   I know my mind is made up.
   So put away your make-up.
   Told you once I won't tell you again.
   It's a crime the way…

Saturday Night Special

Words and Music by Edward King and Ronnie Van Zant

Strum Pattern: 2
Pick Pattern: 2

Verse
Moderate Rock

Additional Lyrics

2. Big Jim's been drinkin' whiskey,
And playin' poker on a losin' night.
Pretty soon big Jim starts a-thinkin'
Somebody been cheatin' and lyin'.
So big Jim commences to fightin',
I wouldn't tell you no lie.
And big Jim done pulled his pistol.
Shot his friend right between the eyes.

3. Hand guns are made for killin',
Ain't no good for nothin' else.
And if you like to drink your whiskey
You might even shoot yourself.
So why don't we dump them, people,
To the bottom of the sea?
Before some fool come around here,
Wanna shoot either you or me.

MCA music publishing

She's So Cold

Words and Music by Mick Jagger and Keith Richards

Strum Pattern: 2
Pick Pattern: 1

Verse
Bright Rock

1. I'm so hot for her, I'm so hot for her, I'm so hot for her, and she's so cold.
2.–5. *See Additional Lyrics*

I'm so hot for her, I'm so hot for her, I'm so hot for her, and she's so cold.

I'm a burn-ing bush, I'm the burn-ing fire, I'm the bleed-ing vol - ca - no.

I'm so hot for her, I'm so hot for her, I'm so hot for her, and she's so cold.

2. Yes, I've she's so cold.
3. Yeah,

Additional Lyrics

2. Yes, I've tried rewiring her, tried refiring her,
I think her engine is permanently stalled.
She's so cold, she so cold,
She so cold, cold, cold like a tombstone.
She's so cold, she's so cold,
She's so cold, cold, cold like an ice cream cone.
She's so cold, she's so cold.
When I touched her my hand just froze.

3. Yeah, I'm so hot for her, I'm so hot for her,
I'm so hot for her, she's so cold.
Put your hand on the heat, put your hand on the heat.
I'm coming on, baby let's go, go.
She's so cold, she's so cold, cold,
She's so cold, but she's beautiful.

4. She's so cold, she's so cold.
I think she was born in an arctic zone.
She's so cold, she's so cold, cold, cold.
When I touched her my hand just froze.
She's so cold, she's so God damn cold,
She's so cold, cold, cold, she's so cold.

5. You were a beauty, a sweet, sweet, beauty.
A sweet, sweet beauty, but stone, stone cold.
You're so cold, you're so cold, cold, cold.
You're so cold, you're so cold.
I'm so hot for you, I'm so hot for you,
I'm so hot for you, and you're so cold.
I'm the burning bush, I'm the burning fire,
I'm the bleeding volcano.
I'm the buring fire, I'm the bleeding volcano…

Substitute

Words and Music by Peter Townshend

Additional Lyrics

2. I was born with a plastic spoon in my mouth.
   The north side of my town faced east and the east was facing south.
   Now you dare to look me in the eye.
   Those crocodile tears I watch you cry.
   It's a genuine problem. You won't try
   To work it out at all; you just pass it by, pass it by.

Suffragette City

Words and Music by David Bowie

Strum Pattern: 2
Pick Pattern: 6
Verse
Medium Rock

1. Hey man, oh leave me a - lone, you know. Hey man, Hen - ry,
2., 3. *See Additional Lyrics*

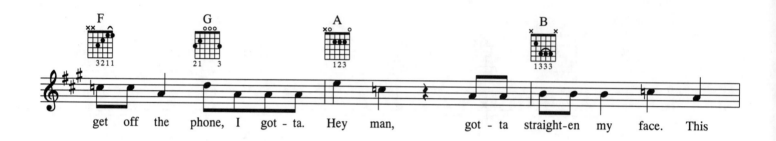

get off the phone, I got - ta. Hey man, got - ta straight-en my face. This

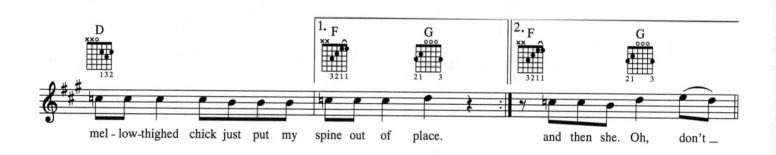

mel - low-thighed chick just put my spine out of place. and then she. Oh, don't __

Chorus

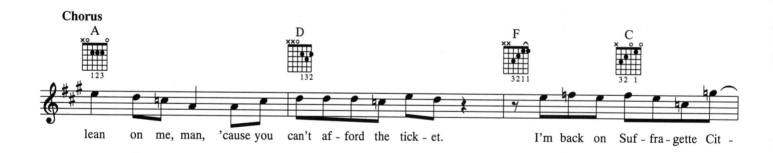

lean on me, man, 'cause you can't af - ford the tick - et. I'm back on Suf - fra - gette Cit -

- y. No, don't lean on me, man, 'cause you ain't got time to check it.

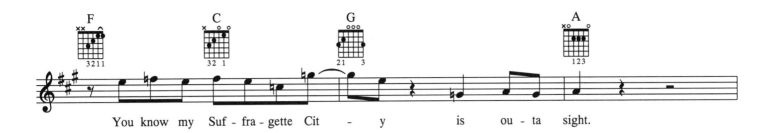

You know my Suf - fra - gette Cit - y is ou - ta sight.

To Coda ⊕

D.C. al Coda
(take 2nd ending)

She's al - right.

⊕ **Coda**

Outro

play 3 times

right. A Suf - fra - gette cit - y.

Suf - fra - gette!

Additional Lyrics

2. Hey man, my school day's insane.
   Hey man, my work's down the drain.
   Hey man, well she's a total blam blam.
   She said she had to squeeze it but she, and then she.

3. Hey man, oh Henry don't be unkind. Go away.
   Hey man, I can't take you this time. No way.
   Hey man, Droogie, don't crash here.
   There's only room for one and here she comes, here she comes.

The Sunshine Of Your Love

Words and Music by Jack Bruce, Pete Brown and Eric Clapton

Strum Pattern: 1

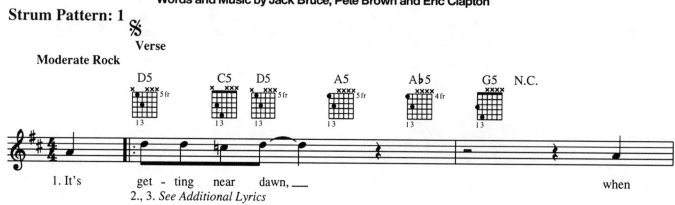

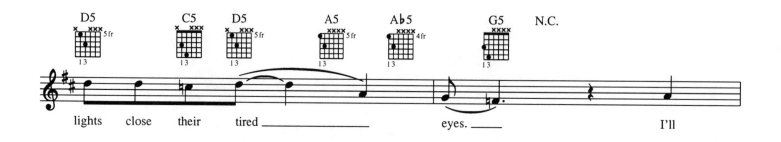

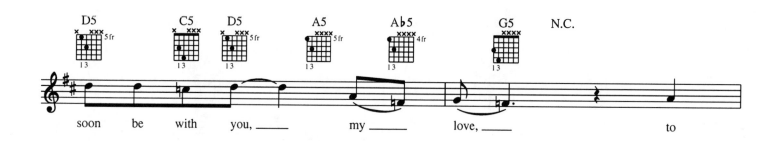

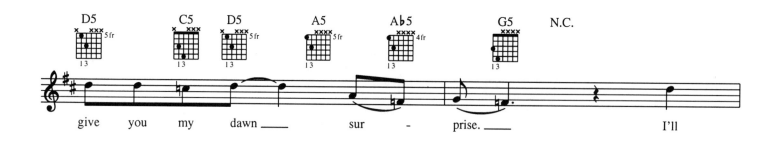

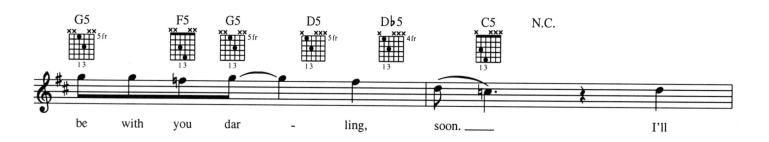

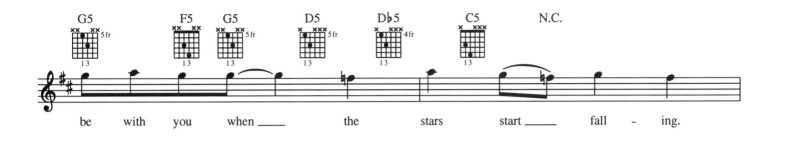

be with you when ____ the stars start ____ fall - ing.

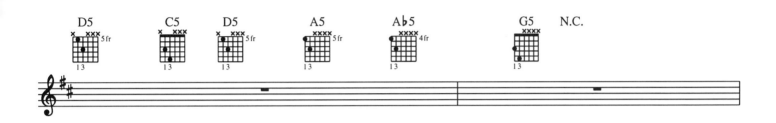

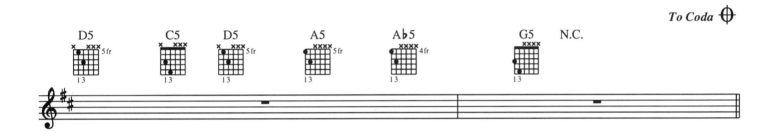

To Coda ⊕

Chorus

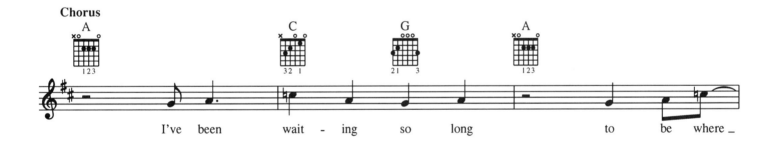

I've been wait - ing so long to be where _

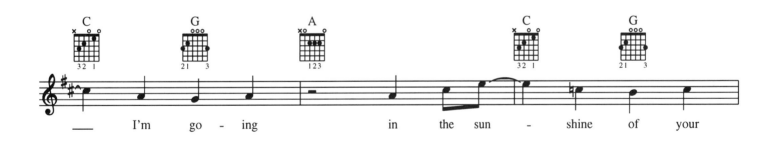

____ I'm go - ing in the sun - shine of your

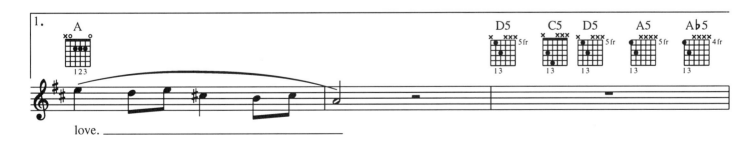

love. _____

⊕ Coda
Outro

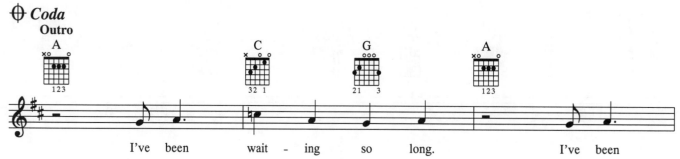

I've been wait - ing so long. I've been

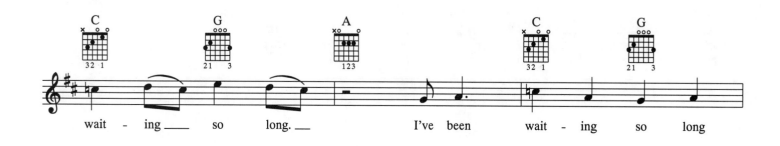

wait - ing ___ so long. ___ I've been wait - ing so long

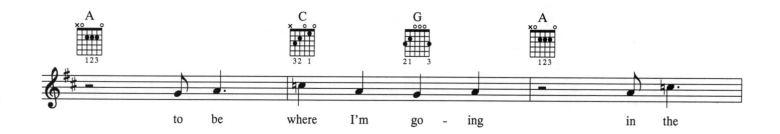

to be where I'm go - ing in the

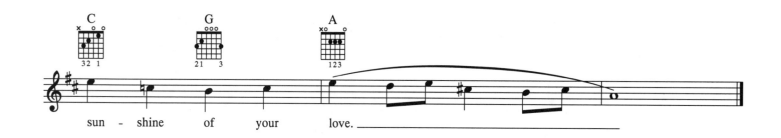

sun - shine of your love. ___

Additional Lyrics

2., 3. I'm with you my love,
The light shining through on you.
Yes, I'm with you my love.
It's the morning and just we two.
I'll stay with you, darling now.
I'll stay with you till my seeds are dried up.

Surrender

Words and Music by Rick Nielsen

Strum Pattern: 2
Pick Pattern: 1
Intro
Moderate Rock

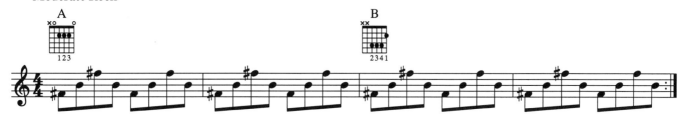

Verse

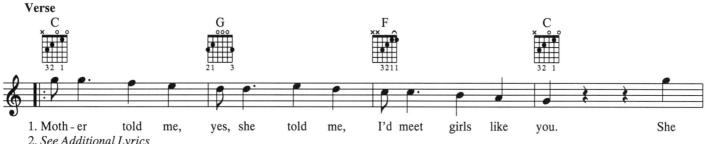

1. Moth - er told me, yes, she told me, I'd meet girls like you. She
2. *See Additional Lyrics*

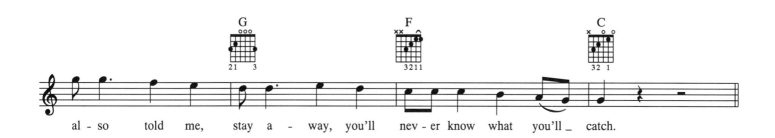

al - so told me, stay a - way, you'll nev - er know what you'll _ catch.

Pre-Chorus

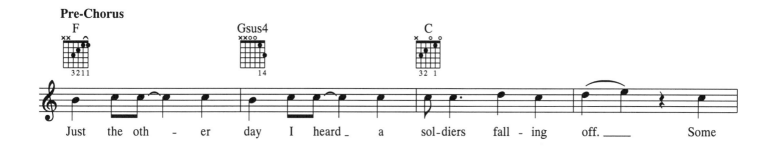

Just the oth - er day I heard _ a sol - diers fall - ing off. ____ Some

In - do - ne - sian junk that's go - ing round. _____

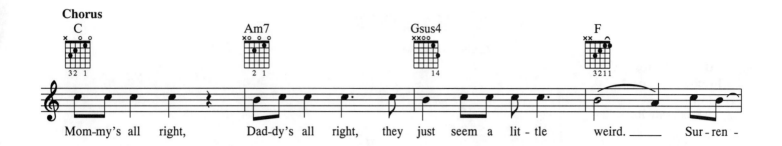

Chorus

Mom-my's all right, Dad-dy's all right, they just seem a lit-tle weird. _____ Sur - ren -

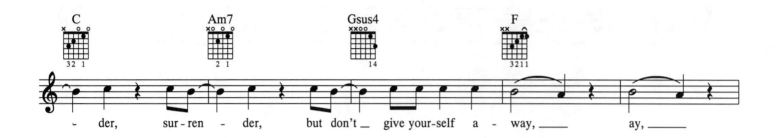

- der, sur - ren - der, but don't _ give your-self a - way, _____ ay, _____

ay, ay.

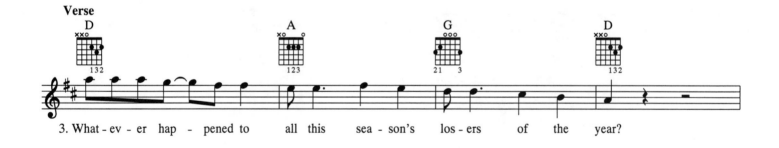

Verse

3. What - ev - er hap - pened to all this sea - son's los - ers of the year?

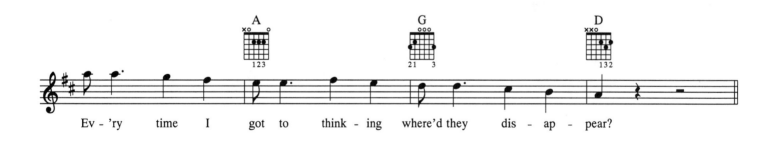

Ev - 'ry time I got to think - ing where'd they dis - ap - pear?

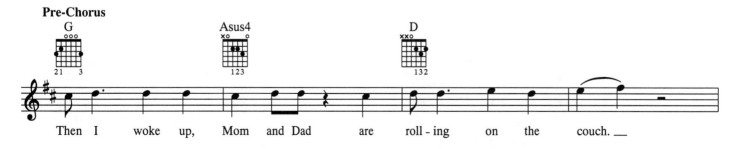

Pre-Chorus

Then I woke up, Mom and Dad are roll - ing on the couch. _

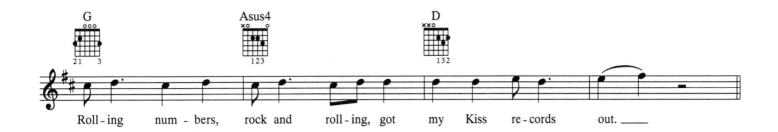

Roll-ing num - bers, rock and roll-ing, got my Kiss re-cords out. _____

Chorus

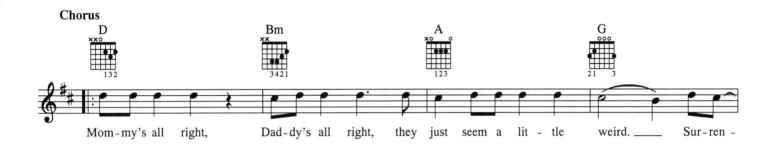

Mom-my's all right, Dad-dy's all right, they just seem a lit - tle weird. _____ Sur-ren -

- der, sur-ren - der, but don't _____ give your-self a - way, _____

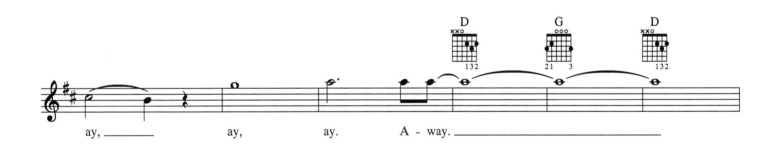

ay, _____ ay, ay. A - way. _____

Repeat and Fade

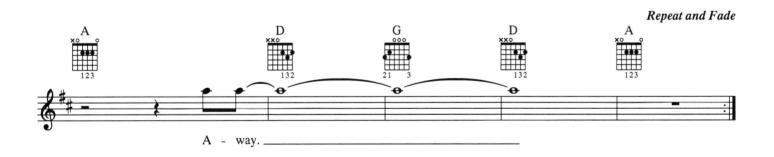

A - way. _____

Additional Lyrics

2. Father says, "Your mother's right, she's really up on things.
Before we married Mommy served in the WACS in the Philippines.
Now I had heard the WACS recruited old maids for the war.
But Mommy isn't one of those, I've known her all these years."

Sweet Home Alabama

Words and Music by Ronnie Van Zant, Ed King and Gary Rossington

Strum Pattern: 2
Pick Pattern: 4

Verse
Moderate Rock

1. Big wheels keep on turn-ing, car-ry me home to see my kin.
2. *See Additional Lyrics*

Sing-ing songs a-bout the south-land, I miss ol' 'bam-y once a - gain. *Spoken: And I think it's a sin.*

Chorus

round an-y-how. Sweet home Al - a - bam-a, where the skies are so

blue. Sweet home Al - a - bam-a, Lord, I'm com-ing home to you.

Verse

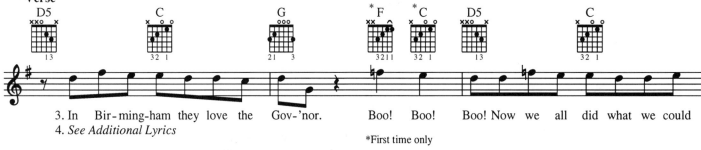

3. In Bir-ming-ham they love the Gov-'nor. Boo! Boo! Boo! Now we all did what we could
4. *See Additional Lyrics*

*First time only

MCA music publishing

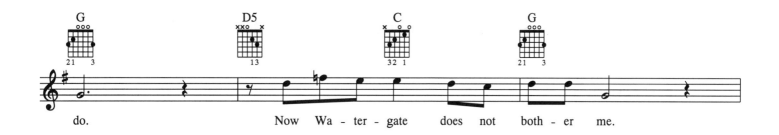

do.   Now Wa - ter - gate does not both - er me.

% Chorus

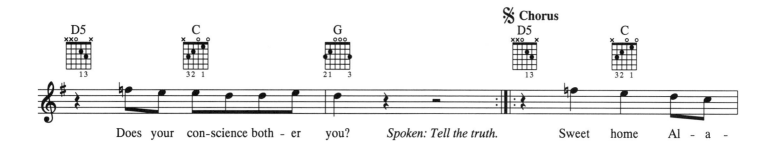

Does your con-science both - er you?   *Spoken: Tell the truth.*   Sweet home Al - a -

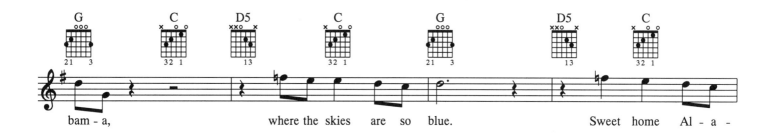

bam - a,   where the skies are so blue.   Sweet home Al - a -

D.S. and Fade

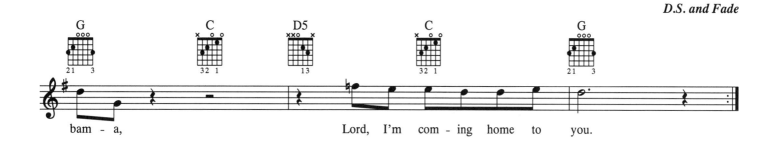

bam - a,   Lord, I'm com - ing home to you.

Additional Lyrics

2. Well, I heard Mister Young sing about her.
   Well, I heard ol' Neil put her down.
   Well, I hope Neil Young will remember,
   A southern man don't need him around anyhow.

4. Now Muscle Shoals has got the Swampers,
   And they've been known to pick a song or two.
   Lord they get me off so much.
   They pick me up when I'm feeling blue.
   Spoken: Now how about you.

Takin' Care Of Business

Words and Music by Randy Bachman

Strum Pattern: 1

Verse
Moderate Rock

1. They get up ev - 'ry morn-ing from the a - larm clock's warn-ing. Take the eight - fif - teen in - to the
2. *See Additional Lyrics*

cit - y. There's a whis - tle up a - bove and peo - ple push-ing, peo - ple shov-ing, and the

girls who try to look pret - ty. If your train's on time you can get to work by nine and

start your slav - ing job to get your pay. __ If you ev - er get an-noyed, look at

me, I'm self - em-ployed. I love to work at noth - ing all day. __ And { I've / we've } been

Chorus

tak-ing care of busi - ness ev - 'ry day. _ Tak-ing care of busi - ness ev - 'ry way. I've been

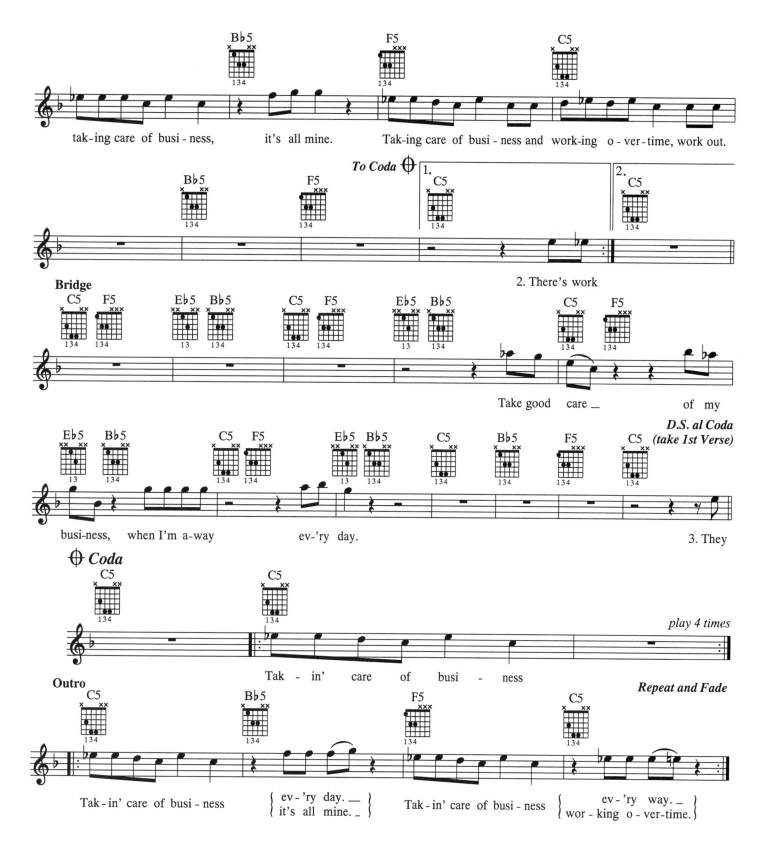

Additional Lyrics

2. There's work easy as fishing,
   You could be a musician
   If you could make sounds loud and mellow.
   Get a second hand guitar,
   Chances are you'll go far
   If you get in with the right bunch of fellows.
   People see you having fun,
   Just a-lying in the sun.
   Tell them that you like it this way.
   It's the work that we avoid
   And we're all self-employed.
   We love to work at nothing all day.

Taxman

Words and Music by George Harrison

Strum Pattern: 2
Pick Pattern: 4

Verse
Moderate Rock

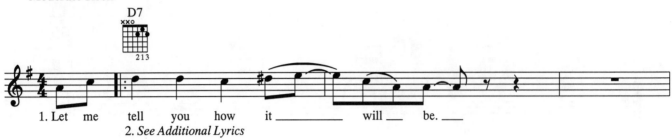

1. Let me tell you how it _____ will ___ be. ___
2. *See Additional Lyrics*

There's one for you, nine-teen for ___ me. ___

Chorus

'Cause I'm the tax-man, yeah, ___ I'm the tax-man. ___

1.

2.

Bridge

___ 2. Should five- If you drive a car, I'll

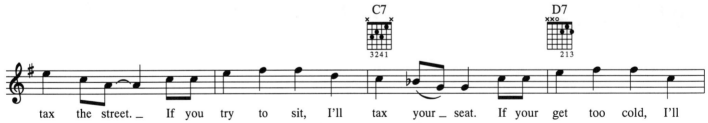

tax the street. ___ If you try to sit, I'll tax your ___ seat. If your get too cold, I'll

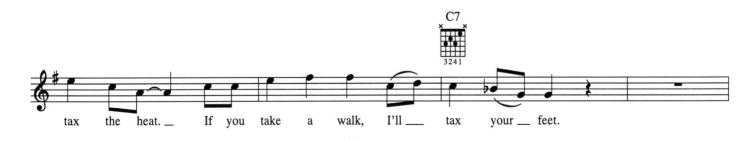

tax the heat. ___ If you take a walk, I'll ___ tax your ___ feet.

Tulsa Time

Words and Music by Danny Flowers

Strum Pattern: 1
Pick Pattern: 1
Verse
Moderate Boogie

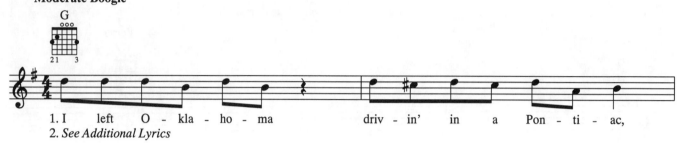

1. I left O - kla - ho - ma driv - in' in a Pon - ti - ac,
2. *See Additional Lyrics*

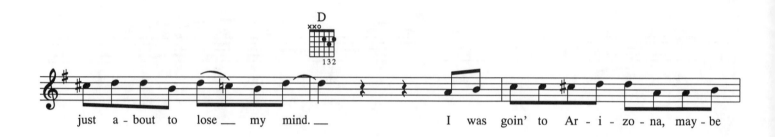

just a - bout to lose __ my mind. __ I was goin' to Ar - i - zo - na, may - be

on to Cal - i - for - nia where the peo - ple all live __ so fine. __ My

ba - by said I's cra - zy. My mom - ma called me la - zy. I was goin' to show 'em all __ this time. _

__ 'Cause you know I ain't no fool 'n' I don't need no more school - in'. I was

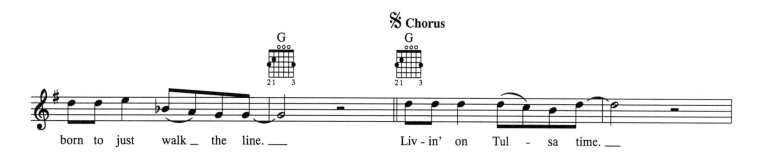

born to just walk __ the line. ___   Liv - in' on Tul - sa time. __

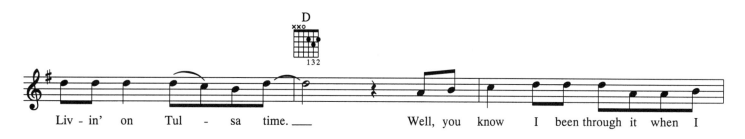

Liv - in' on Tul - sa time. ___   Well, you know   I been through it when I

set my watch back to it.   Liv - in' on   Tul - sa time. __   2. Well __

Additional Lyrics

2. Well there I was in Hollywood,
   Wishin' I was doin' good,
   Talkin' on the telephone line.
   But they don't need me in the movies
   And nobody sings my songs,
   Where the guess I'm just a wastin' time.
   Well, then I got to thinkin',
   Man, I'm really sinkin'
   And I really had a flash this time.
   I had no bus'ness leavin' and nobody would be grievin'
   If I went on back to Tulsa time.

Chorus Livin' on Tulsa time.
   Livin' on Tulsa time.
   Gonna set my watch back to it,
   Cause you know I've been through it,
   Livin' on Tulsa time.

Tumbling Dice

Words and Music by Mick Jagger and Keith Richards

Strum Pattern: 2, 3
Pick Pattern: 1

Intro   Verse
Moderate Rock

1. Wom-en think I'm tast-y but they're al-ways tryin' to waste me and make

me burn the can-dle right down. But ba-by,

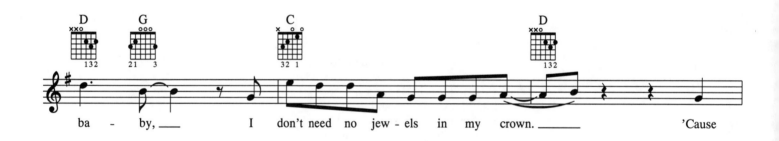

ba-by, I don't need no jew-els in my crown. 'Cause

all you wom-en is low down gam-blers, cheat-in' like I don't know how. But

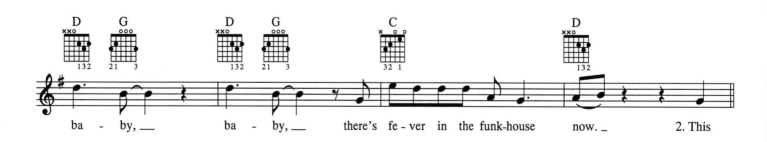

ba-by, baby, there's fe-ver in the funk-house now. 2. This

Verse

G

low down bitch-in' got my poor feet a-itch-in', you know, __ you know the deuce is still wild. __

D **G** **D** **G**

__ Ba - by, __ I can't stay, __ you got to

Chorus

C

roll _____ me and call me the tum - blin' __ dice. _____

Verse

G

3. Al - ways in a hur - ry, I nev - er stop to wor - ry, don't you see the time flash-in' by. __

D **G** **D** **G**

_____ Hon - ey, __ got no mon - ey, __ I'm all

C **D** **G**

six - es and sev - ens and nines. _____ Say now, ba - by, I'm the

rank out - sid - er, you can be my part - ner in crime. _____ But

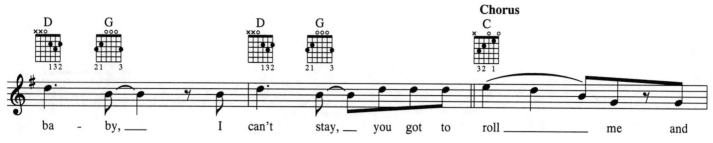

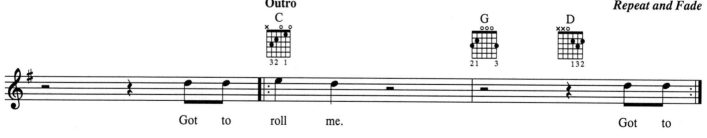

We Will Rock You

Words and Music by Brian May

Strum Pattern: 1
Pick Pattern: 2

Verse
Moderate Rock

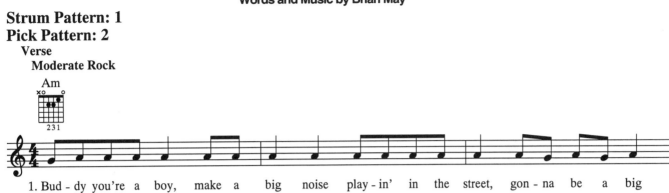

1. Bud - dy you're a boy, make a big noise play - in' in the street, gon - na be a big
2., 3. *See Additional Lyrics*

man some day. You got mud on yo' face. You big dis - grace. Kick - in your can all

Chorus
Am

o - ver the place sing-in', "We will, we will rock you.

1., 2.
We will, we will rock you."

3.
rock you."

Additional Lyrics

2. Buddy you're a young man, hard man shoutin' in the street,
   Gonna take on the world some day.
   You got blood on yo' face.
   You big disgrace.
   Wavin' your banner all over the place singin',

3. Buddy you're an old man, poor man pleadin' with your eyes,
   Gonna make you some peace someday.
   You got mud on your face.
   You big disgrace.
   Somebody better put you back into your place singin',

Up On Cripple Creek

Words and Music by Robbie Robertson

Strum Pattern: 1
Pick Pattern: 2

drunk - ard's dream _ if I ev - er did see one. _____

Bridge

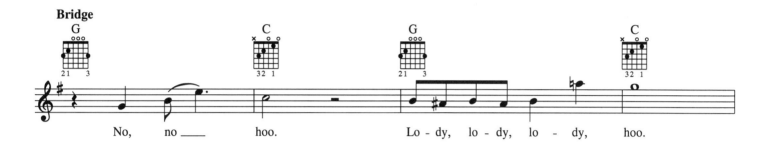

No, no _____ hoo. Lo - dy, lo - dy, lo - dy, hoo.

D.S. al Coda
(take 3rd ending)

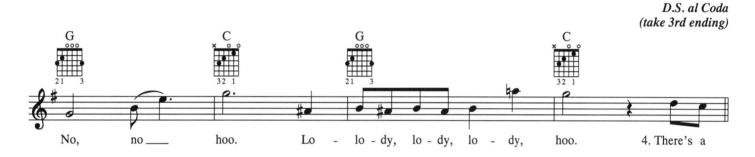

No, no _____ hoo. Lo - lo - dy, lo - dy, lo - dy, hoo. 4. There's a

$\bigoplus$ *Coda*   **Outro**   *Repeat and Fade*

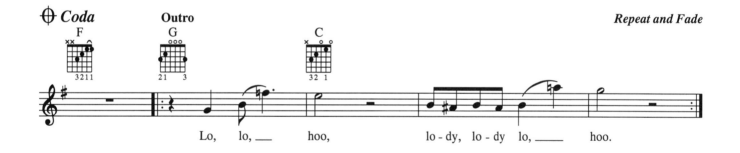

Lo, lo, _____ hoo, lo - dy, lo - dy lo, _____ hoo.

Additional Lyrics

2. Good luck had just stung me,
   To the race track I did go.
   She bet on one horse to win
   And I bet on another to show.
   The odds were in my favor.
   I had 'em five to one.
   And that nag to win came around the track,
   Sure enough, she had won.

3. I took up all of my winnings,
   And I gave my little Bessie half.
   She tore it up and threw it in my face
   Just for a laugh.
   Now, if there's one thing in the whole wide world
   I sure would like to see,
   That's when that little love of mine
   Dips her donut in my tea.

4. There's a flood in California
   And up north, it's freezin' cold,
   And livin' on the road
   Is getting pretty old.
   So I guess I'll call up my big mama,
   Tell her I'll be rollin' in.
   But you know deep down I'm kinda tempted,
   To go see my Bessie again.

Walk On The Wild Side

Words and Music by Lou Reed

Strum Pattern: 4
Pick Pattern: 5

Doo, doo, doo, doo, doo, doo, doo, doo, doo, doo, doo, doo. Doo, doo, doo, doo, doo, doo, doo, doo, doo, doo, doo, doo.

Doo, doo, doo, doo, doo, doo, doo, doo, doo, doo, doo, doo. Doo, doo, doo, doo, doo, doo, doo, doo, doo, doo, doo, doo.

wild   side."

wild   side."   And the   col-ored girls   say:

Outro

play 4 times

Doo, doo, doo, doo, doo, doo, doo, doo, doo, doo, doo, doo. Doo, doo, doo, doo, doo, doo, doo, doo, doo, doo, doo, doo."

Additional Lyrics

2. Little Joe never once gave it away.
   Ev'rybody had to pay and pay.
   A hustle here and a hustle there.
   New York City is the place where they said,

3. Sugar Plum Fairy came and hit the streets,
   Lookin' for soul food and a place to eat.
   Went to the Apollo,
   You should have seen 'em go, go, go. They said,

4. Jackie is just speedin' away.
   Thought she was James Dean for a day.
   Then I guess she had to crash.
   Valium would have helped that bash. She said,

Walk This Way

Words and Music by Steven Tyler and Joe Perry

Strum Pattern: 6
Pick Pattern: 4

Verse
Moderate Rock

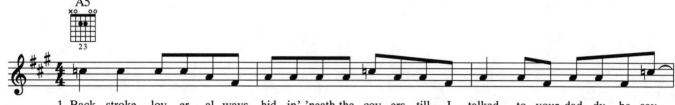

1. Back - stroke lov - er al - ways hid - in' 'neath the cov - ers till I talked to your dad - dy he say.

He said, "You ain't seen noth - in' till you're down on a muf - fin then you're

sure to be a - chang - in' your ways." I met a cheer - lead - er, was a

real young bleed - er, oh, the times I could rem - i - nisce; 'cause the

best things of lov - in' with her sis - ter and her cou - sin on - ly start - ed with a lit - tle

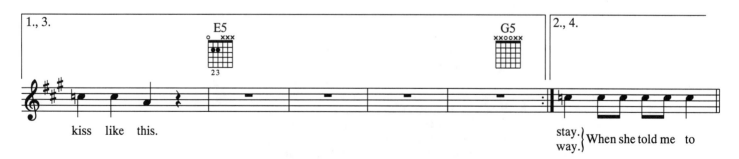

1., 3.

kiss like this.

2., 4.

stay.}
way.} When she told me to

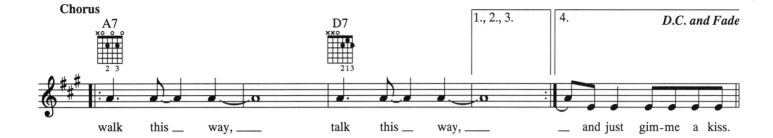

walk this ___ way, ___ talk this ___ way, ___ ___ and just gim-me a kiss.

Additional Lyrics

2. Seesaw swinger with the boys in the school and your feet flyin' up in the air.
   Singin', "Hey, diddle, diddle, with your kitty in the middle of the swing like you didn't care."
   So I took a big chance at the high school dance with a missy who was ready to play.
   Was it me she was foolin' 'cause she knew what she was doin', when I knowed her love was here to stay.

3. School girl sweeties with a classy kinda sassy little skirts climbin' way up their knee.
   There was three young ladies in the school gym locker when I noticed they was lookin' at me.
   I was a high school loser, never made it with a lady till the boys told me somethin' I missed.
   Then my next door neighbor with a daughter had a favor, so I gave her just a little kiss.

4. Seesaw swinger with the boys in the school and your feet flyin' up in the air.
   Singin', "Hey, diddle, diddle, with your kitty in the middle of the swing like you didn't care."
   So I took a big chance at the high school dance with a missy who was ready to play.
   Was it me she was foolin' 'cause she knew what she was doin', when she told me how to walk this way.

You Really Got Me

Words and Music by Ray Davies

Strum Pattern: 1

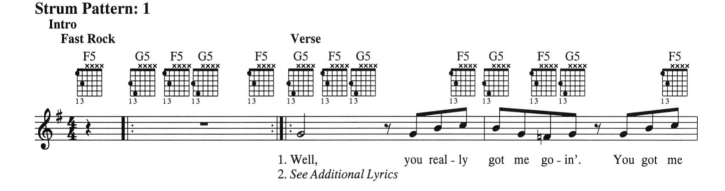

1. Well, you real-ly got me go-in'. You got me
2. *See Additional Lyrics*

so I don't know what I'm do-in'. Yeah, you real-ly

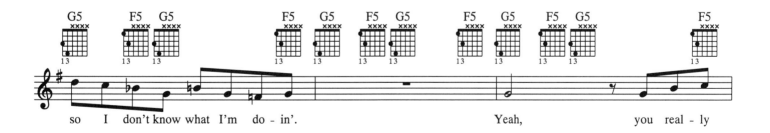

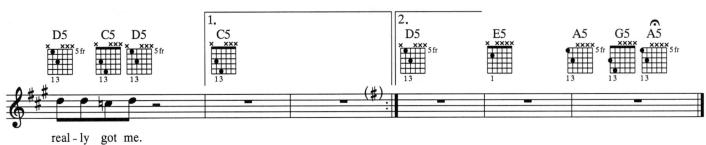

Additional Lyrics

2. See, don't ever set me free.
   I always want to be by your side.
   Yeah, you really got me now.
   You got me so I can't sleep at night.

Whatever Gets You Through The Night

Words and Music by John Lennon

Strum Pattern: 1
Pick Pattern: 1

Intro
Moderately Fast

1. What-ev-er gets you through the night 'sal-right, 'sal-right.

2., 3. *See Additional Lyrics*

It's your mon-ey or your life 'sal-right, 'sal-right. Don't need a sword to cut through

flow-ers. Oh, no, oh, no.

2. What-ev-er gets you through your

Chorus

Hold me dar-lin', come on lis-ten to ___ me, I won't do you no harm.

Trust me dar-lin', come on lis-ten to ___ me, come on lis-ten to ___ me, come on lis-ten, lis-ten.

Interlude

D.S. and Fade
(take 2nd ending)

3. What-ev-er gets you to the

Additional Lyrics

2. Whatever gets you through your life,
   'Salright, 'salright.
   Do it wrong or do it right,
   'Salright, 'salright.
   Don't need a watch to waste your time.
   Oh no, oh no.

3. Whatever gets you to the light
   'Salright, 'salright.
   Out of the blue or out of sight,
   'Salright, 'salright.
   Don't need a gun to blow your mind.
   Oh no, oh no.

We Are The Champions

Words and Music by Freddie Mercury

*Strum Pattern: 8
*Pick Pattern: 8

Moderately Slow

Verse

*play 2 times per meas.

1. I've paid my dues, _____ time af - ter time.
2. *See Additional Lyrics*

I've done my ____ sen - tence but com - mit - ted no crime. ____

And bad mis - takes, I've made a few.

I've had my share of sand kicked in my face but I've come

through. And I need to go on, and on, and on, and on.

% Chorus

We ____ are the cham - pions ____ my friend. _____ And

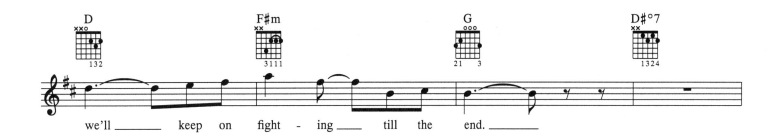

we'll ____ keep on fight - ing ____ till the end. _____

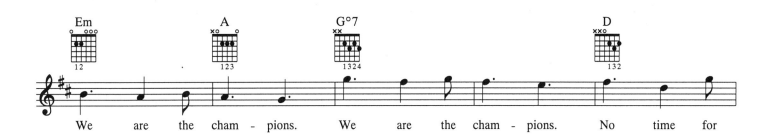

We are the cham - pions. We are the cham - pions. No time for

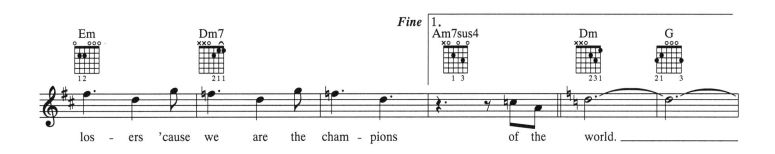

los - ers 'cause we are the cham - pions of the world. _____

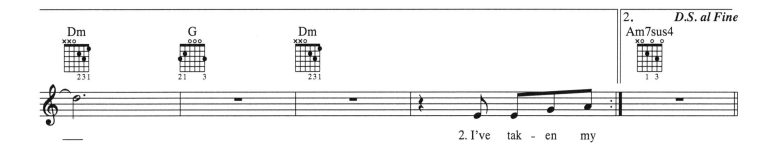

____ 2. I've tak - en my

Additional Lyrics

2. I've taken my bows
   And my curtain calls.
   You brought me fame and fortune and ev'rything that goes with it,
   I thank you all.
   But it's been no bed of roses,
   No pleasure cruise.
   I consider it a challenge before the whole human race
   And I ain't gonna lose.

A Whiter Shade Of Pale

Words and Music by Keith Reid and Gary Brooker

Strum Pattern: 1, 3
Pick Pattern: 2, 3

Verse
Slow Rock

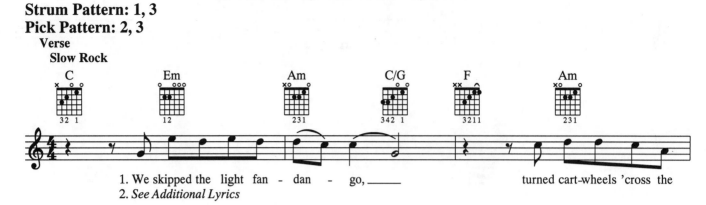

1. We skipped the light fan-dan-go, _____ turned cart-wheels 'cross the
2. *See Additional Lyrics*

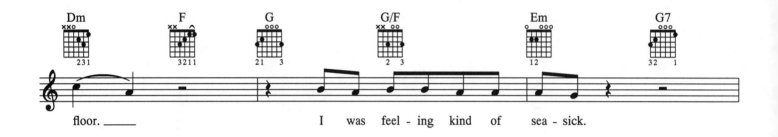

floor. _____ I was feel-ing kind of sea-sick.

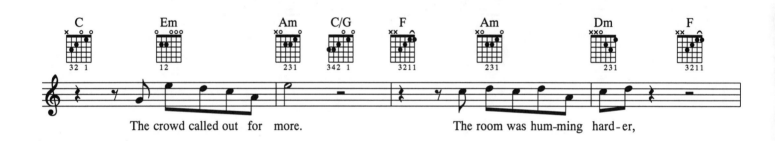

The crowd called out for more. The room was hum-ming hard-er,

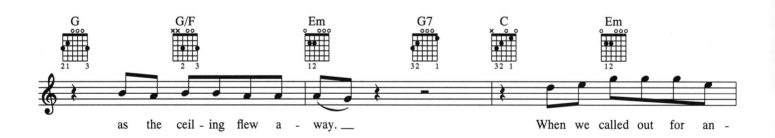

as the ceil-ing flew a-way. _____ When we called out for an-

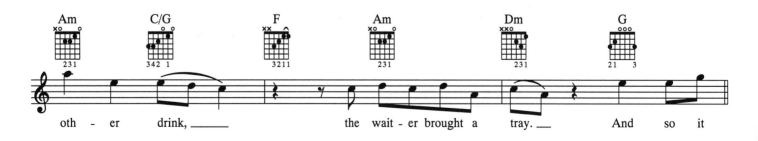

oth-er drink, _____ the wait-er brought a tray. _____ And so it

Chorus

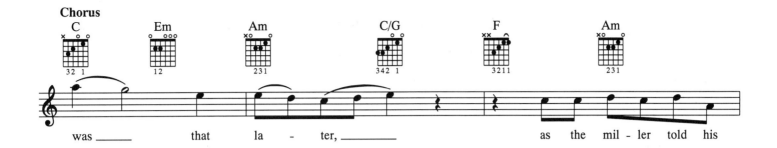

was _____ that la - ter, _____ as the mil - ler told his

tale, _____ that her face at first just ghost - ly, turned a

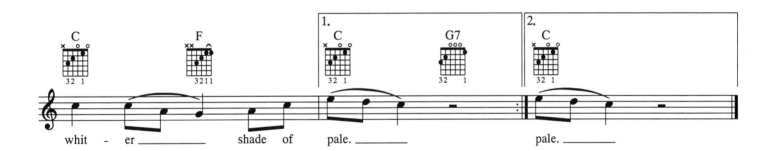

whit - er _____ shade of pale. _____ pale. _____

Additional Lyrics

2. She said, "There is no reason,
   And the truth is plain to see."
   But I wandered through my playing cards,
   And would not let her be
   One of sixteen vestal virgins,
   Who were leaving for the coast.
   And although my eyes where open,
   They might just as well have been closed.

You Ain't Seen Nothin' Yet

Words and Music by Randy Bachman

Strum Pattern: 1
Pick Pattern: 1

Intro
Moderate Rock

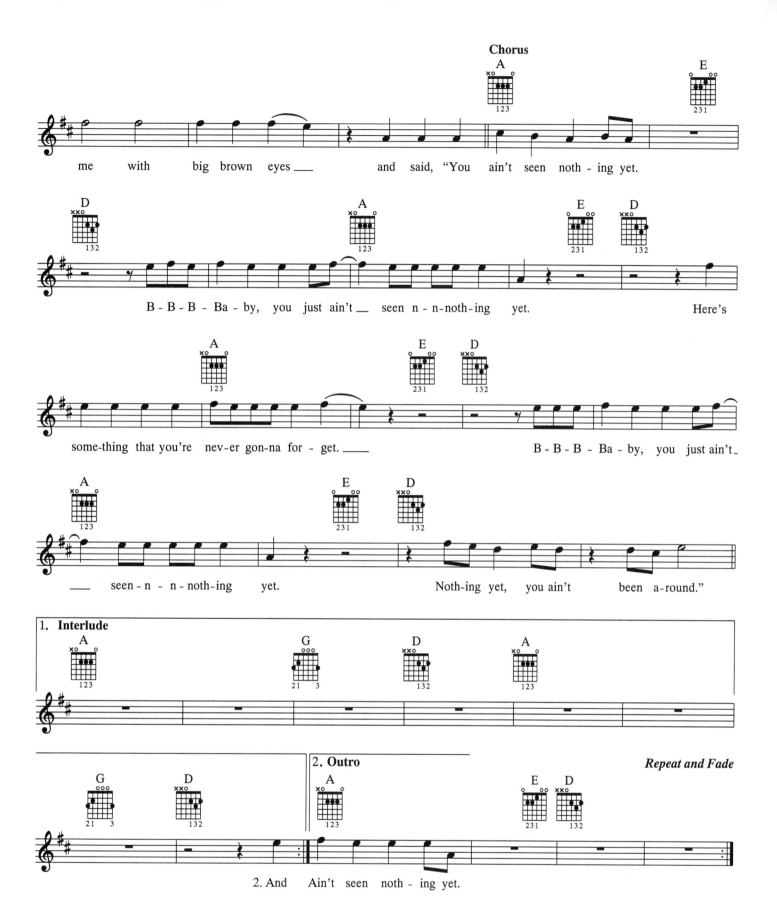

Wild Thing

Words and Music by Chip Taylor

Strum Pattern: 5
Pick Pattern: 1

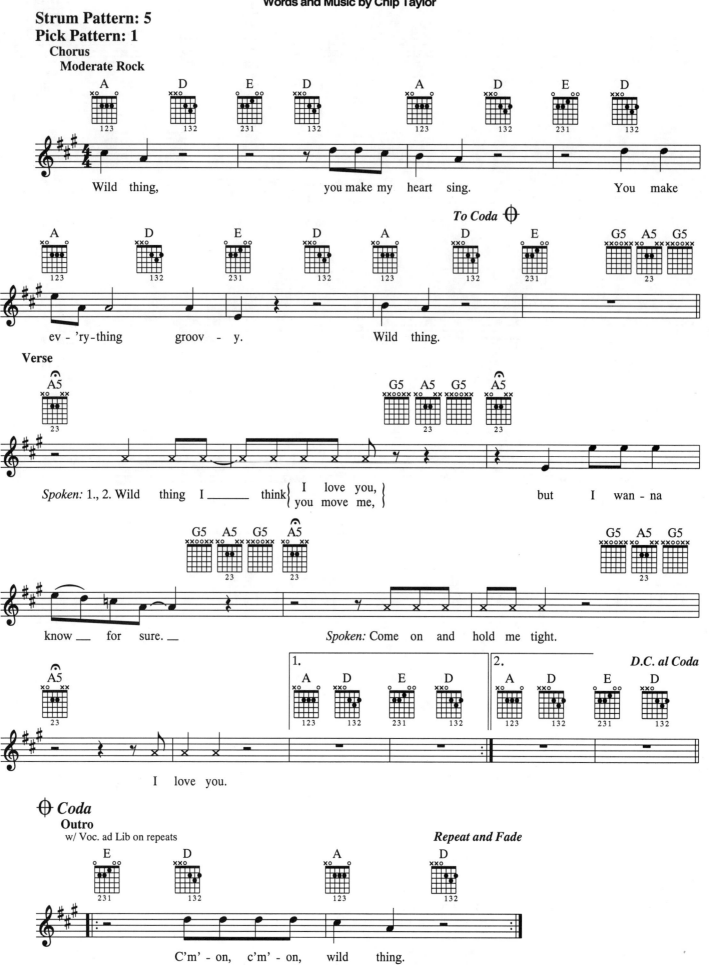

WITH NOTES AND TAB

This series features simplified arrangements with notes, tab, chord charts, and strum and pick patterns.

The Best Of Aerosmith

20 of their hits, including: Dream On • Livin' On The Edge • Love In An Elevator • Sweet Emotion • Walk This Way • and more.
00702001 . . . . $12.95

The Big Christmas Collection

35 all-time favorites, including: Go Tell It On The Mountain • The Greatest Gift Of All • Happy Holiday • I'll Be Home For Christmas • Jingle-Bell Rock • The Most Wonderful Time Of The Year • O Holy Night • Silver And Gold • and more.
00698978 . . . . $14.95

Eric Clapton's Best

17 classics arranged for easy guitar, including: After Midnight • I Shot The Sheriff • Layla • White Room • Wonderful Tonight • and more.
00702090 . . . . $12.95

Eric Clapton – Unplugged

All 14 songs from his best-selling acoustic album, featuring: Hey Hey • Layla • Nobody Know You When You're Down And Out • Tears In Heaven • and more.
00702086 . . . . $10.95

Contemporary Christian Favorites

20 great easy guitar arrangements of contemporary Christian songs, including: El Shaddai • Friends • He Is Able • I Will Be Here • In The Name Of The Lord • Love In Any Language • Love Will Be Our Home • Say The Name • Thy Word • Via Dolorosa • and more.
00702006 . . . . $9.95

Contemporary Country Ballads

15 easy favorites, including: Fast Movin' Train • The Greatest Man I Ever Knew • I Never Knew Love • Rumor Has It • She Is His Only Need • Ghost In This House • and more.
00702091 . . . . $9.95

Contemporary Country Pickin'

21 easy country classics, including: Boot Scootin' Boogie • Chasin' That Neon Rainbow • Chattahoochee • Papa Loved Mama • Straight Tequila Night • and more.
00702089 . . . . $9.95

The Best Of Def Leppard

12 songs that even beginners can play! Songs include: Bringin' On The Heartbreak • Hysteria • Pour Some Sugar On Me • Photograph • Rock Of Ages • and more.
00702084 . . . . $12.95

Disney Movie Hits

10 fun favorites for beginning guitar players, including: Be Our Guest • Beauty And The Beast • Under The Sea • A Whole New World • and more.
00702085 . . . . $9.95

Gospel Favorites For Guitar

An amazing collection of 50 favorites, including: Amazing Grace • Did You Stop To Pray This Morning • He Lives • His Name Is Wonderful • How Great Thou Art • The King Is Coming • My God Is Real • Nearer, My God, To Thee • The Old Rugged Cross • Take My Hand, Precious Lord • Turn Your Radio On • Will The Circle Be Unbroken • and more.
00699374 . . . . $14.95

Guitar Wedding Collection

Over 50 contemporary sentimental favorites, including: All I Ask Of You • Dedicated To The One I Love • Don't Know Much • Grow Old With Me • Longer • My Funny Valentine • Somewhere Out There • Through The Years • Unchained Melody • When I'm Sixty-Four • and more!
00699394 . . . . $14.95

The New Best Of Billy Joel

15 songs, including: All About Soul • It's Still Rock And Roll To Me • Just The Way You Are • The River Of Dreams • Uptown Girl • We Didn't Start The Fire • and more.
00702087 . . . . $9.95

The New Best Of Elton John

17 of his best, including: Bennie And The Jets • Candle In The Wind • Don't Go Breaking My Heart • Goodbye Yellow Brick Road • Your Song • and more.
00702088 . . . . $9.95

Best Of Carole King For Easy Guitar

25 easy arrangements of her hits: I Feel The Earth Move • It's Too Late • (You Make Me Feel Like) A Natural Woman • Some Kind Of Wonderful • Up On The Roof • Will You Love Me Tomorrow • You Light Up My Life • and more.
00702011. . . . . $12.95

Rockin' Elvis For Easy Guitar

15 legendary hits, including: All Shook Up • Blue Suede Shoes • Don't Be Cruel • Hound Dog • Return To Sender • and more.
00702004 . . . . $9.95

The Best Of Queen For Guitar

19 simplified classics, including: Another One Bites The Dust • Bohemian Rhapsody • Crazy Little Thing Called Love • We Will Rock You • You're My Best Friend • and more.
00699415 . . . . $12.95

The Best Of The Rolling Stones

13 classics, including: Angie • Emotional Rescue • Hang Fire • It's Only Rock 'N' Roll • Start Me Up • Waiting On A Friend • and more.
00702092 . . . . $9.95

The Rolling Stones Collection

28 of their best, including: Angie • Beast Of Burden • Hang Fire • It's Only Rock 'N' Roll (But I Like It) • Start Me Up • Tumbling Dice • Waiting On A Friend • and more.
00702093 . . . . 17.95

FOR MORE INFORMATION, SEE YOUR LOCAL MUSIC DEALER, OR WRITE TO:

HAL•LEONARD
CORPORATION
7777 W. BLUEMOUND RD. P.O. BOX 13819 MILWAUKEE, WI 53213

0795

THE GUITAR TECHNIQUES SERIES

The series designed to get you started! Each book clearly presents essential concepts, highlighting specific elements of guitar playing and music theory. Most books include tablature and standard notation.

Acoustic Rock For Guitar

The acoustic guitar has found renewed popularity in contemporary rock. From ballads to metal, you'll find many artists adding that distinctive acoustic sound to their songs. This book demonstrates the elements of good acoustic guitar playing – both pick and fingerstyle – that are used in rock today. Topics include Chords and Variations, Strumming Styles, Picking Patterns, Scales and Runs, and much more.
00699327....................................$6.95

Basic Blues For Guitar

This book taps into the history of great blues guitarists like B.B. King and Muddy Waters. It teaches the guitarist blues accompaniments, bar chords and how to improvise leads.
00699008 ....$6.95

Music Theory For Guitar

Music theory is the cornerstone in understanding music. But how does a guitar player relate it to the guitar? This volume answers that question. Concepts of scale, harmony, chords, intervals and modes are presented in the context of applying them to the guitar. This book will open the door to not only understanding the fundamentals of music, but also the world of playing the guitar with more insight and intelligence.
00699329....................................$7.95

Finger Picks For Guitar

A convenient reference to 47 fingerstyle guitar accompaniment patterns for use with all types of music. In standard notation and tablature. Also includes playing tips.

00699125....................................$6.95

Lead Blues Licks

This book examines a number of blues licks in the styles of such greats as B.B. King, Albert King, Stevie Ray Vaughan, Eric Clapton, Chuck Berry, and more. Varying these licks and combining them with others can improve lead playing and can be used in rock styles as well as blues. Clearly written in notes and tab, you'll progress from the standard blues progression and blues scale to the various techniques of bending, fast pull offs and hammer-ons, double stops, and more.
00699325....................................$6.95

Lead Rock Licks For Guitar

Learn the latest hot licks played by great guitarists, including Jeff Beck, Neal Schon (of Journey), Andy Summers (Police), and Randy Rhoads (Ozzy Osbourne). The guitarist can use each lick in this book as building material to further create new and more exciting licks of their own.
00699007 ....$6.95

Rhythms For Blues For Guitar

This book brings to life everything you need to play blues rhythm patterns, in a quick, handy and easy-to-use book. Everything from basic blues progressions to turnarounds, including swing, shuffle, straight eighths rhythms, plus small, altered and sliding chord patterns. All are presented in the style of many of the great blues and rock blues legends. Includes notes and tab.
00699326....................................$6.95

Extended Scale Playing For Guitar

An innovative approach to expanding left hand technique by Joe Puma. The sliding first finger technique presented in this book will give players a new and broader outlook on the guitar. The book explores a variety of scales – major, minor, half-tone/whole-tone – and more.
00697237....................................$7.95

Right Hand Techniques

Through basic alternate, sweep and cross picking patterns, 10 chord arpeggios, palm muting and fingerstyle techniques, this book presents everything you need to know in getting started with the basic techniques needed to play every type of music. Additional topics include rhythm, rake and fingerstyle techniques. A real power packed technique book!
00699328....................................$6.95

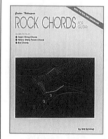

Rock Chords For Guitar

Learn to play open-string, heavy metal power chords and bar chords with this book. This book introduces most of the chords needed to play today's rock 'n' roll. There are very clear fingering diagrams and chord frames on the top of each page. Empty staves at the bottom of each page allow the player to draw in his own chord patterns.
00689649 ....$6.95

Rock Scales For Guitar

This book contains all of the Rock, Blues, and Country scales employed in today's music. It shows the guitarist how scales are constructed and designed, how scales connect and relate to one another, how and where to use the scales they are learning, all of the possible scale forms for each different scale type, how to move each scale to new tonal areas and much, much more.
00699164 ....$6.95

Strums For Guitar

A handy guide that features 48 guitar strumming patterns for use with all styles of music. Also includes playing tips.
00699135 ....$6.95